Praise for *Manifesting Made Easy*

"Jen Mazer is truly the Queen of Manifestation. She has a gift for breaking down the manifestation process into fun, easy-to-implement steps. This book will help you live out your biggest dreams."
—Marci Shimoff, #1 *New York Times* bestselling author of *Happy for No Reason*

"Thank you, Jen. I love you. You're a soul sister."
—Janet Bray Attwood, *New York Times* bestselling author of *The Passion Test*

"You've probably heard that 'success leaves clues.' And when a woman is one of the most sought-after speakers and trainers on manifestation of this millennium, I'd say that's a big enough clue that you should run (not walk) and grab a copy of the book where she's put all of her wisdom and tools together in one place. I love Jen Mazer, as she has contributed to my life in more ways than I can count. But what I admire about her most is that she absolutely knows the formula for powerful manifestation—and after you read this book, you will, too."
—Debra Poneman, bestselling author and founder of Yes to Success Seminars, Inc.

"I know who to call if I get stuck. Because every now and then you need a refresher to remind you of what you know. If I need to remember, I'm gonna call the Queen of Manifestation."
—Rickie Byars Beckwith, world-renowned singer and musical director of Agape International Choir

MANIFESTING
Made Easy

How to Harness the Law of Attraction
to Get What You Really Want

JEN MAZER

Foreword by Dr. Joe Vitale, bestselling author of *The Awakened Millionaire*

Adams Media
New York London Toronto Sydney New Delhi

Dedication

This book is dedicated to all of the dreamers.
And to my little dreamer, Nailah.

Adams Media
An Imprint of Simon & Schuster, Inc.
100 Technology Center Drive
Stoughton, MA 02072

For information about special discounts for bulk purchases, please contact Simon & Schuster Special Sales at 1-866-506-1949 or business@simonandschuster.com.

The Simon & Schuster Speakers Bureau can bring authors to your live event. For more information or to book an event contact the Simon & Schuster Speakers Bureau at 1-866-248-3049 or visit our website at www.simonspeakers.com.

Interior images © iStockphoto.com/aleksandarvelasevic

Manufactured in the United States of America

6 2022

Library of Congress Cataloging-in-Publication Data has been applied for.

ISBN 978-1-4405-9704-6
ISBN 978-1-4405-9705-3 (ebook)

Acknowledgments

First and foremost, thank you for reading this book. You are a part of a global movement of people moving through the world in a new way of being, manifesting with ease. Thank you for consciously co-creating with me.

There are so many people who helped make this book a reality. So much gratitude to my friend Caits Meissner, who first gave me the name Queen of Manifestation. Little did you know the ripple effect you would have! Thank you Alicia Jean-Noel for hosting my very first manifestation workshop.

Thank you Elisa Albert for introducing me to the world of writing. Thanks Terra Chalberg, my phenomenal literary agent. You've always had my best interest at heart. Thank you Tyla Fowler for helping me organize my ideas for the book. Thank you Katie Corcoran Lytle, my amazing editor. You've been a joy to work with. Thanks Rebecca Tarr Thomas. Without you, this book wouldn't have been written. You had a vision, and you knew my voice needed to be heard. Thank you Rachel Barbic for being my right-hand woman in my business. To Megan Stark, thank you for coming onboard.

Dad, thank you for your unwavering support, gentleness, and positivity throughout my life. Mom, thank you for always being there, for cultivating my artistic nature, and for supporting my wild adventures. You've both always told me to go for my dreams. Thank you for your constant love and belief in me. Debra, thanks for showing me how to be authentically alive and in touch with my spirit. Grandma Bernice, you continue to inspire me with your positive outlook on life and your ability to overcome any obstacle. I hope I'm doing yoga at ninety! I love you. Thank you to all my teachers and mentors over the years, especially Maric

Forleo, Fabienne Frederickson, Susie Carder, Rha Goddess, Sonia Choquette, Gay Hendricks, Jack Canfield, Dr. Brian Weiss, Reverend Michael Beckwith, and Peggy McColl.

Bob Wolter, your life was an inspiration. Thanks for being my prom date.

Gabriela Seiders, thank you for telling me to go to New York.

Judith Shepherd, you sparked my love for literature. Thank you.

Thanks to all the experts who I've interviewed as a part of my Manifesting with the Masters Summit. Our talks have not only inspired me, but thousands of others.

Thank you to the luminaries whose work has influenced me throughout the years, especially Frida Kahlo, Amma, Oprah, Paramahansa Yogananda, Albert Maysles, Yoko Ono, Deepak Chopra, Louise Hay, and Nelson Mandela.

Wynton Marsalis, the House of Tribes, John Zorn, Kiki Smith, and all my neighbors on Seventh Street—my time there was magical. Thank you for inspiring me to live my dreams through your example.

Linda Vega, you were the best college advisor I could have asked for. Thank you for encouraging me to apply for the honors trip to Senegal. It was the beginning of many life-changing trips to Africa.

Roselee Goldberg, thank you for your mentorship.

Sylvia Rascon, thanks for telling me to go to India to get my yoga teacher's certification.

Thank you Stephanie Diamond for your constant reflection of my gifts.

Jo-Na Williams, Mia Moran, Lainie Love Dalby, Amy Walton Groome, and Alex Jamieson, thank you for your encouragement and accountability.

Maya Azucena, Shannon Mulkey, Angie Dykshorn, Cara Mia Harris, Christina Trush, Matt Kneller, Lindsey Sharp, Teresa

Weber, Adrienne Sapione, and Anne Hayman, thank you for your belief in me.

Lisa Rueff, thank you for being a light in my life and for sparking so much fun.

Rickie Byars Beckwith, Janet Attwood, Marci Shimoff, Debra Poneman, and Dr. Joe Vitale, thank you for your kind words.

I want to thank all my clients around the world. Your stories and successes keep me going. Working with you is a true joy. I want to especially thank Robin Green, Michelle Cleary, and Star Staubach for allowing me to share your inspiring success stories. I am grateful to be able to do this work.

All my Manifestation Masters—you know who you are. Thank you for trusting me as your guide and opening up to your magnificence. Leading you through this process made writing this book so easy!

To my soul family, Kute, Dagger, and Jahman, thank you for allowing my heart to open even more. Kara Bernarda and Serena Falasconi, I am grateful for our soul sister adventures. Haridas, thank you for being my family in India. Mpumi, my brother from a South African mother, I love you. Ben Harper, thank you for your presence in my life and for showing me that magic is real.

Amayo, you're a wonderful partner and father. Your love and support during this whole process means the world to me. Thank you for teaching me about commitment, practice, and nurturing your craft. I love you.

Nailah, thank you for choosing me as your mom. You're the ultimate blessing in my life. I love you with all my heart. You're my greatest teacher and inspiration.

Contents

Join the Manifestation Movement

You are a part of a movement of people manifesting their ideal lives with greater ease than ever before. And in order to help you stay in a positive mindset while you manifest, I've created a global community online at www.facebook.com/groups/manifesteasy/. It's a place to connect with other like-minded people who are going for their dreams. And it's completely free to join.

I've also compiled extra resources, meditations, and free bonuses to enhance your manifestation journey on my website at www.queenofmanifestation.com.

Stay connected and #manifestit.

Share your success stories and tag me @jenmazer with the hashtag #manifestingmadeeasy on social media.

And now, enjoy the ride.

Foreword

When it comes to manifesting what you want, why are so many people confused? Why do so many people feel frustrated? Why do so many not get the results they want?

In my decades of writing and speaking about how to create your life the way you prefer, I notice that people have an incomplete understanding of the manifestation process.

Many think you just "sit and think" your desires into reality. Others think all you have to do is "wait around" for your manifestation to materialize. And still others don't believe any of this "mind stuff" actually works.

What's the truth?

What does work?

How can you really and truly manifest your heart's desires?

I'm happy to report that you can find the answers in *Manifesting Made Easy*. I've read it and love it. It simplifies the process of manifestation so anybody can get it and do it. I finally have a resource I can send people to when they ask me about manifestation—and that resource is this book.

I personally know Jen. She interviewed me twice for her manifestation series. She's smart, upbeat, open-minded, and on a mission to help people—to help you. I'm honored that she asked me to write this foreword and even more excited for you—because you can finally understand how to manifest whatever you want, beginning with the turn of a page.

Expect miracles.

Dr. Joe Vitale, bestselling author of *The Awakened Millionaire*
www.MrFire.com

Introduction

"The biggest adventure you can
take is to live the life of your dreams."

Oprah, talk show host, philanthropist, and founder of the OWN Network

Congratulations! You're about to experience a new level of ease and awareness in your life. This book will change the way you show up in the world, and how the world shows up for you.

Welcome to a new way of being. Take a moment and imagine right now that you had unlimited resources. You could do, have, experience, and become anything that your heart desires. What if you were in the flow, being completely supported and guided by the universe? What if you were in touch with your intuition, knowing at each moment that the next opportunity would present itself, and the next one, and the next one? You would show up and be taken care of and everything would work out exactly as you wanted it to—because you manifested it.

It's possible.

Chances are, you're reading this book because you haven't already manifested everything you want in your life. You may know about manifestation, but do you know all the principles and the right order to put them into practice? Are you wondering if you're doing this manifestation thing right? Perhaps you're already experiencing some successes, but you feel a pull for a bigger dream within you. But over-efforting to manifest something bigger has led to burnout and anxiety.

Forget about hustling or pushing to manifest your desires. That approach is old and stale. You see, most people overcomplicate the manifesting process, but it's actually quite simple once you understand how it works and what steps you need to take to allow your dreams to unfold. Whether you're a novice or an experienced manifestor, *Manifesting Made Easy* will teach you a fresh way to embrace what's in your heart and call it into your life. You see, the more you push to make things happen, the harder it will be. The more you can open up and allow in the things that you desire, the easier it will be to manifest. And I'm going to show you how.

Now, who am I anyway? Well, my friends actually gave me the nickname Queen of Manifestation because I've always been able to dream up outrageous adventures and actually live them out—from living rent-free in Manhattan's East Village for more than 10 years and traveling the world to paying off more than $38,000 of debt in less than a year. I've become friends with my favorite mentors and artists, from Hollywood directors to spiritual teachers. I manifested the man of my dreams and gave birth to a beautiful girl at home. My work has been featured in the *New York Times*, *Huffington Post*, and *New York* magazine. I help people manifest their deepest desires.

Many of my clients come to me because, while they understand the basics of manifesting, they've lost their momentum. They don't know what to do and they want to get back into alignment.

Some come to me to learn what manifestation is and how to use it. Others come to me to manifest a bigger dream for themselves. They've already accomplished a lot, but have a desire within them to expand. And nothing makes me happier than when I see a client's life transform through our work together. My clients have manifested their first $60,000 months, TEDx Talks, book deals, new homes, marriages, improved health, and successful businesses that are changing the world—and I can help you do the same.

You see, I believe that simply having a dream in the first place means that it wants to emerge through you and is meant for you. In *Manifesting Made Easy*, I take you on an easy, fun, and effective journey of uncovering those hidden dreams and manifesting them through personal stories and practical exercises. Here you'll learn how to get out of your own way and open up to your full potential. You'll clear limiting beliefs, discover what you really want, and create new habits to support you in experiencing infinite abundance and joy. And really, you're the only one stopping your dream from emerging. It's up to you to open up to what wants to come in. Are you ready for love, wealth, health, and success? How about that big creative project you've always wanted to finish (or start!)?

We're all naturally born manifestors. Anything is possible for you. If you can imagine it, you can create it. Knowing that you create your own life, wouldn't you want to create the best life you could possibly dream up?

This is your moment. This is your turning point. This is your transformation. Congratulations.

How to Use This Book

So now that you know you'll be learning how to manifest your desires throughout the book, let's talk about how you can get the most out of my manifestation knowledge. Here we'll go over what you'll find in each entry, how to use it, and how you can take your manifestation skills to the next level. So let's take a look at how the entry structure will help you manifest your dreams.

What You'll Find

Throughout the book, I've made sure that each entry is organized in a way that will allow you to get the most of your manifestation. In each entry you'll first learn an easy lesson that will teach you about a very important factor of manifestation. These simple lessons show you how to take action and make sure manifestation is front and center in your everyday life as you work to achieve your goals and realize your dreams.

Once you've been given the information on the importance of the lesson, you'll find ways to apply that lesson to your real life in the "How to Apply It" section of each entry. This text will give you tips on how to apply the manifestation principles in your life and help ensure you're taking the steps you need to reach your goals.

And for you serious manifestors, I have included "Advanced Manifesting Tips" with some of the entries. These tips are for readers who want to take their manifestation journey further. Just as in a yoga class, you can choose to apply these advanced practices if you'd like to deepen your practice.

Learn in Order

Each lesson builds upon the last. So follow along, apply the lessons, and you'll be well on your way to manifesting your dream life.

I consciously designed the book so that you can experience progressive growth and change if you read each lesson in order and apply the techniques I provide. This is the exact same process I've led my Manifestation Master students through for the past five years that I've been teaching manifestation. First I "Demystify" the manifestation process so you know exactly how manifestation really works. Then I help you get clear on your "Dream" so that the universe understands what you want to manifest. In "Dare" I teach you the exact process for taking action in a way that's in alignment with your vision. But once you've taken action, limiting beliefs tend to show up to stop you from continuing with the process. That's exactly why "Discover" comes next. You'll understand exactly what's stopped you from manifesting before, and then you'll "Detach" from those things in order to manifest with more ease. This part where you detach is crucial to your success. We end the book with "Delight," where I show you more advanced practices so that you can delight in your dreams realized.

From my years of teaching manifestation in my online programs and private coaching, I know that if you apply each lesson, you'll experience positive change. But if you skip around, you may miss an important step in the manifestation process.

Keep an Open Mind and Commit

I invite you to keep an open mind while you read this book. A lot of these lessons appear simple. But it's in the application of the principles that you truly experience a new reality. You might be one of those people who reads a lot of self-help books, nodding along with recognition, "Yes, yes, exactly!"

Listen, I'm one of those people too.

But are you actually applying what you're reading? If you really want to experience results, then I encourage you to commit to learning the lessons and doing the exercises I share in this book. Right now is your opportunity to take an active part in co-creating your life.

And when I say co-create, I mean that we're truly co-creating with the universe. Part of you is dreaming up what's possible for you. And the universe also holds a vision for you. It's sort of like a meeting of the minds. You take one step forward, and the universe meets you halfway. But you must take that first step.

Create a Manifestation Journal

The best way to incorporate all of these lessons and commit to achieving your dreams is to create a manifestation journal. This is a place where you'll record anything related to your dreams. You'll also use this to answer the prompts throughout this book. If you don't have a journal nearby, you can get out a piece of paper and a pen, but I encourage you to create a separate journal that's special to your manifestation journey.

When you write things down, you integrate the teachings even more. In addition, the act of writing helps increase your intuition and the awareness of the support that is already there for you. Your manifestation journal is a place where you'll record your dreams, express your gratitude, notice synchronicities, and answer questions from the "How to Apply It" sections of the book. I'll also be giving you advanced journaling techniques you can use to enhance the flow of manifestation. This is your sacred space to record anything you want. It's for your eyes only. Feel free to choose a journal that makes you feel good and represents the future you that you are manifesting.

Embrace Change

Instead of being afraid of what change may look like, I invite you to embrace it. Go with the flow of life. Once you can find alignment with the natural laws of the universe, you'll experience such lightness, such pure joy and happiness, you'll wonder why it took so long to realize how you've been stopping yourself before.

There's a reason you were called to buy this book. There are no coincidences in life, only delicious synchronicity.

So let's begin!

Part 1

DEMYSTIFY:
HOW DOES MANIFESTATION ACTUALLY WORK?

"Your imagination is a preview of your life's coming attractions."
Albert Einstein, physicist

Have you been disappointed with manifestation before? Aren't sure it works or how it's even possible? Well, I'm here to demystify the manifestation process!

The first thing you need to understand is how manifestation works and why you may have had mixed results in the past. This foundational understanding is crucial for consciously manifesting what you want in your life. The truth is that we're all manifesting whether we realize it or not. You're currently creating your own reality. But if you don't understand the process, then you'll attract all sorts of random things to you that may or may not match your desires. And you won't ever be satisfied with what's showing up for you.

With conscious manifestation, you truly can have, be, and experience all that you desire. You co-create with the universe. Here you'll learn all about the science of manifestation and where it all begins. You'll soon realize that everything is energy and you're connected to the entire universe. There are universal laws that are working on your behalf all the time. Manifestation is a lot simpler than you think. If you can reconnect to the essence of who you truly are, magic unfolds. And it all starts with your imagination and opening up to possibility.

Imagine

"Everything you can imagine is real."
Pablo Picasso, twentieth-century artist

All of manifestation comes from imagination.

Consider this for a minute: Your dreams chose you for a reason. They want to emerge through you.

What if everything you've always thought was only your imagination—mere fantasy—is actually you intuiting what's to come? What if you were actually meant to have and experience everything you've ever dreamed up for yourself? How differently would you act? How would you walk through the world? With confidence, ease, and grace?

I think the reason that I'm such a good manifestor is that I'm an artist. I view my life as my canvas. When I was little, I would carry around a sketchbook all the time. I saw the world in my mind and drew it. First I would get the idea for what I wanted to create, and then I would actually create it. My artwork has since been published in the *New York Times* and reviewed in major publications. I dreamt it all up first.

That's what I want for you. You see, the secret to manifestation is that your dreams truly want to emerge through you. They're in your head for a reason. But it's up to you to decide if you want to follow through with your inspiration. You can! You wouldn't have that idea if it weren't possible to actually manifest it. It's your *choice* to manifest it.

Before this book came into reality, it was just an idea. It did not exist, but the possibility for it existed in my imagination. In fact, I knew I wanted to write a book but hadn't really owned my desire. Then one day I said it out loud: "There's a book within me." That's it. I shared my dream. I claimed it. And it was literally two weeks later that my publisher actually reached out to *me* to write it. People told me, "That never happens!" Oh, but it does. That same possibility for your dreams already lives inside of you. And once you understand how easy manifesting can be, there will be a quickening between idea and reality. It'll be like you're magnetizing your dreams.

Most people don't dream big enough. And that's the first way they limit themselves. If you don't believe you'll be able to do something, you won't. It's that simple. But if you can expand your capacity for what you believe is possible for yourself, then you open up the possibility for even greater success and abundance.

How to Apply It

Close your eyes and begin to allow yourself to imagine that you could be, have, or do anything you want. If you had unlimited resources and you knew that the universe was on your side, what would you be doing with your life? Where would you be living? Who would be in your life? What would be fun for you to create and experience?

In this part of the process, anything goes. Nothing is too outrageous for you. You're simply using your imagination to get an understanding of your desires. What is it that you want right now? It may look different than what you thought you wanted before. That's okay, too. Just allow yourself to imagine your dream life.

Advanced Manifesting Tip

See if you can make your dream life even bigger. Can you amplify your vision in any way? Imagine what it would feel like to be completely supported by the entire universe. Allow your dream to grow.

Use the Law of Attraction

"It's not your work to make anything happen. It's your work to dream it and let it happen. Law of Attraction will make it happen. In your joy, you create something, and then you maintain your vibrational harmony with it, and the Universe must find a way to bring it about."

Abraham-Hicks, master universal teacher

What you ask for, you receive.

To really learn how to manifest your dreams, you need to understand a little bit about the law of attraction. The law of attraction means: ask and it is given. You attract things to you that match what you're putting out. Like a radio, you transmit an energetic signal and receive matching signals from the universe in response. Simply put, the law of attraction says that your thoughts create your reality. What you think about, comes about. It's a universal law.

Now, if that sounds pretty far out there, let's take a look at another scientific law of the universe that is widely accepted as true: Newton's law of gravity. Newton's law states that any two bodies in the universe attract each other with a force that is directly proportional to the product of their masses and inversely proportional to the square of the distance between them. In other words, if you let go of this book, it will fall to the ground. You can't see the gravitational force, but you can feel its effects. The law of attraction is the same. It's a universal law just as real as gravity. You might not be able to see it, but it's there, and it's always in effect.

Even if you're skeptical about how this works, allow yourself to play with the thought. For just a moment, open yourself to the possibility that your thoughts are creating your reality. You're probably saying, "If my thoughts are creating my reality, then why aren't I experiencing what I want?" Well, if it were as simple as saying, "I'm a millionaire," and then becoming one, everyone would be rich.

What you say is just part of the equation. There are layers of beliefs beneath the surface. As is the case for many of us, those hidden layers are the ones stopping you from getting what you truly want. Your thoughts aren't in alignment with what you desire.

Pam Grout, the *New York Times* bestselling author of *E-Squared*, actually leads readers through experiments that they test on themselves to prove that our thoughts create our reality. There is one in the book where readers are instructed to plant green bean seeds in an empty egg carton. They're asked to talk positively to the left half of seeds, and negatively to the seeds on the right, while watering them equally every two days with the positive expectation that the seeds on the left will grow faster. And guess what? It's been found over and over again that the ones that were talked to positively and expected to grow faster, *did* grow faster. What do you tell yourself on a daily basis?

Imagine that you're at a restaurant and you're about to place an order for something to eat. You decide you want pizza. So you tell the waiter that you'd like to order the pizza. But when the waiter leaves, you can't stop thinking about how great that Kale Caesar Salad sounded. And you start to question your decision to order the pizza. Plus pizza isn't that healthy for you anyway, right? And you begin to feel guilty for ordering it. You think to yourself that it's going to make you fat. You always indulge. You really should go on a diet. It's not going to be that good anyway. You flag down the waiter and tell her you want to cancel your order. But they've already started to make the pizza. If you flag down the waiter and keep changing your order, the kitchen (or in this case, the universe) doesn't know what to bring you. By having all of these thoughts, whether you're aware of them or not, you're sending mixed messages to the universe. No matter what you choose to order, you must decide what you want, and feel good about your decision.

You say you want something. You recite affirmations, positive statements affirming you already have what you're longing for. But on the inside, you don't truly believe it's possible. You doubt it's going to happen anyway. Or you think you don't really deserve it. So you convince yourself that you aren't sure if it's what you really want. We all have these thoughts at moments. I'm going to help you get out of that cycle so that you can stay in a high vibration while you're manifesting.

The law of attraction states that you attract things that match the vibration you put out into the world. So you want your vibration to be positive in order to attract more positive experiences into your life.

How to Apply It

When I was traveling in Los Angeles, I discovered these neat little Universe Order Pads at a gift store. They look like the order pads waiters carry with them in a restaurant, but they're meant to be filled out for fun. So I want you to put your order into the universe now. In your manifestation journal, create a list titled "My Order to the Universe" and then write down five things you're asking for without putting "I want" in front of them. Simply write your order. For example, your list could look like the following:

My Order to the Universe:

1. A new car
2. An amazing relationship
3. A successful career
4. A child
5. To be financially free

The simpler, the better for this exercise. What are five things you want to manifest right now?

Cultivate Possibility

"Ordinary people believe only in the possible. Extraordinary people visualize not what is possible or probable, but what is impossible. And by visualizing the impossible, they begin to see it as possible."

Chérie Carter-Scott, New York Times *bestselling author and life coach*

When an idea shows up that feels as if it's outside of the realm of possibility, allow yourself the opportunity to fully indulge in the "What if?"

I'm an artist and my love is a musician. In raising our daughter, we are constantly reinforcing her belief that she can create anything she dreams up. So she does! She gets an idea to create something—from a cardboard guitar to a doll swing made from a jewelry stand—and together, we make it. We open up to the possibility of it happening simply because she has the idea for it. We never shut her down, because we know how important it is to cultivate possibility.

But if you're like most people, somewhere along the way, someone told you that what you imagined wasn't possible. You were given a reason why you couldn't create or achieve something, and you believed it. Perhaps that reason is still lingering deep beneath the surface as a limiting belief—a small voice repeating in your head that "you can't." Maybe that voice says:

- You're not good enough.
- You'll get hurt.
- You don't know what you're doing.

- People won't like you.
- It will never work.

In Part 4, you'll learn how to discover your limiting beliefs and more importantly, how to clear them. But for now, start believing that regardless of what that voice says, anything is possible simply because the idea comes into your mind in the first place. Your dreams chose you. The fact that you've imagined them means that it's possible to attain them. You just need to cultivate that feeling of possibility.

So the next time a wild idea pops into your head—for instance, "I want to write a book"—you could react in a few different ways:

- **Shut off all possibility.** You could think, "Oh, I could never do that," and let it go.
- **Allow a glimmer of possibility that is quickly sidelined.** You could think, "That's a cool idea!"
- **Cultivate possibility.** You say to yourself, "Wow, I'm writing a book! How cool is that!" You could get excited about the possibility of writing the book. You could allow yourself to believe that you're actually becoming an author. Picture yourself writing the book. Then imagine seeing a book with your name on it on the shelf of your favorite bookstore

Can you sense how different these reactions feel in your body? When you come from a place of cultivating possibility, your ideas come from a place of trust. You know that you've been given the idea because it's already happening. When you trust your visions, you can step into them. And once you do, it's a lot easier to take action on your dreams.

Every time you have a new idea, you're in fact shaping your new reality, but it also means that if you're currently in a "bad" mood, you have the ability to change it. You don't need to blame anyone. You can simply choose to believe the situation will change, and in doing so, you've already affected the situation. If you think the situation will get better, you're helping it get better.

There's a famous study of electrons from Israel's Weizmann Institute of Science which proved that "the greater the amount of 'watching,' the greater the observer's influence on what actually takes place." We know that an object doesn't exist independently of the observer. Your actual attention and intention affect the object itself. In other words, the more aware you are of your thoughts, the more you will affect the outcome of your thoughts.

Not only do the possibilities for your dreams live inside of you, but the fact that you're imagining them in the first place means that they already exist. In other words, you already have what you're imagining. When you cultivate possibility, you trust that simply having the idea means it's happening. So manifesting is more about allowing what's already there for you to come in, versus pushing to try to manifest it. It's an exercise in trust and receiving.

How to Apply It

The next time an idea pops into your head, pay attention to how you respond. If you notice any "I could never do that" thoughts coming up, acknowledge them, and then make the conscious choice to respond differently.

For now, simply change your "I could never" or "I can't" to "How can I?" This way, instead of closing off all possibility for your dreams, you open up space for them to emerge. Opening up to possibility is simply telling yourself, "Hmm, that's an interesting idea. I wonder how that could happen?" instead of saying, "Hmm, that's an interesting idea, and it could never happen." Your dream *can* come true if you cultivate the possibility for it. You're probably familiar with the expression, "Where there's a will, there's a way." Well, the way always exists. At this stage, don't be concerned with the *how* for your dreams. It will appear. Focus on the *what*, knowing that whatever you dream up is possible to manifest.

Partner with the Universe to Create Your Dreams

"We are tiny patches of the universe looking at itself—and building itself."

John Wheeler, physicist

We're not just observers of our lives. We're participants.

According to theoretical physicist John Wheeler, we live in a "participatory universe"—an idea that strongly influenced Wheeler's contribution to the field of quantum physics, the branch of physics that uses quantum theory to describe and predict the properties of a physical system. In a nutshell, quantum theory says that everything is energy and your thought waves influence particles of matter. If you expect a certain result, you're actually encouraging that result to emerge physically. This is good news in terms of manifestation. There's an infinite field of possibility and potentiality in the universe that we influence with our thoughts. We're actually creating our reality in every moment.

We're not just observers of our lives. We're participants. Or, as I like to think of it, it means we're co-creating with the universe. This goes back to the concept that when you imagine something, it's partly you coming up with a new idea, but it's also you intuiting an idea that the universe is sending out.

Every time you have a new idea, you're in fact shaping your new reality, but it's not just that your thoughts are creating your reality. You need to assume the feelings of your dreams already being fulfilled. For example, if you want to be wealthy, you want to do things that make you feel wealthy now. You could go to your favorite upscale store and try on clothes that make you feel wealthy. You could even buy something for yourself to take home and wear to feel abundant. By focusing your energy on what it feels like to have what you desire, you send a clear message to the universe. And the universe is a reflection of your thoughts. It's always saying, "Yes, thank you for your order. Received and delivered." And if you are able to act on the ideas coming to you, you'll be able to manifest your desires into physical existence. For example, you keep thinking about taking a particular class and then you receive an e-mail about a new opportunity to study with a teacher you've been wanting to in a class that just happens to be in your neighborhood. Those are signs from the universe showing you the *how* to manifest your desires. But you must be an active participant. You have to take action on the ideas the universe gives you. The universe will keep talking to you if it knows you're paying attention.

You see, the truth is, you're never doing anything alone.

Part of the quantum theory is the idea that there's a hidden web connecting all of life. We may think we're separate from the universe, but in fact, we are all part of the same universal field. If you were to take a microscope and look at your atoms, you'd see that they're constantly moving and vibrating. When you look even closer, you can't really tell where one thing ends and another begins. All the atoms are moving and rotating around one another. What appears separate is actually all connected. We're all participating in the global consciousness of the planet. We are like a rainbow in which you can't tell where one color ends and another begins.

Similarly, your thoughts don't only affect you, they also affect other people. Think about a time when you've walked into a room and felt overwhelming negative energy. Someone you've come in contact with has bad vibes and you can feel it. This phenomenon doesn't only happen on an individual level; it also occurs on a global level. Major catastrophes are felt all over the world through ripples of sadness or fear. On the flip side, there've been global days of peace and prayer that have been scientifically studied for their positive effects on the behavior of people who are entirely unconnected to the peaceful actions. According to a Washington crime rate study, there was a 23 percent decrease in crime due to meditation during a three-week period in Washington D.C., where 4,000 people meditated on peace. The police commissioner had previously said the only way to reduce crime by 20 percent would be to have 20 inches of snow! And interestingly, the crime rate increased as soon as the meditation ended.

There's a lot of science to prove how manifesting works. But how can you apply it in everyday life? And what happens when something comes into the picture that throws you off? You see, you have the power to manifest whatever you want because the universe is a *yes* universe; it's a mirror of your thoughts and it's always supporting you and wanting you to step into your greatness. The universe is saying yes to whatever we speak or think, either positive or negative.

For example, think of the last time you had a bad day. You spill your coffee. Your child throws a temper tantrum. You miss your train to work. You get to work and discover you've missed an important meeting. How could you have forgotten? You're in a downward spiral. While it may seem inevitable, a downward spiral can in fact be turned around.

It starts with your mindset. If, when you spill your coffee, you tell yourself, "I'm having a bad day," you're going to continue the cycle of having a bad day. Remember, the universe is a mirror. If you say you're having a bad day, you will receive more evidence to support that belief. Instead, try saying something like, "Oops, I spilled my coffee." Then forgive yourself. Let it go. It doesn't have to set the tone of your entire day unless you allow it to. *You* get to choose. So many people are simply unaware of how they participate in this cycle. But this is a participatory universe.

This is how manifestation really works: You attract things to you based on the vibration that you're giving out. So if you're thinking positive thoughts and feeling confident, if you really believe that things are happening *for* you, you start to notice that good things are coming to you. You notice that synchronicities are occurring. Amazing opportunities are showing up because you're expecting them to.

When you come from a place of trust and inner knowing, you can stay in alignment despite any external circumstances. You don't have to push to bring your dreams into being. You simply open up to them and allow them to come in. Once you know what you desire, the next step is to open up to what the universe wants to emerge through you. This feels more like a gentle pull toward something bigger than yourself. There's a marriage of the two: universe and you.

How to Apply It

To understand how you participate with the universe, take out your manifestation journal and divide a page into three columns.

At the top of the first column write, "What I want from the universe." At the top of the second column write, "What the universe wants from me." At the top of the third column write, "What the universe and I want together." For example:

What I Want from the Universe	What the Universe Wants from Me	What the Universe and I Want Together
To be a successful artist	To create with ease	To be a creator and manifest on the physical realm
To be happy and free	To be happy and free	To be happy and free
To spend more time with my family	To enjoy each moment of my life	To love

Go through one column at a time, starting with what you want from the universe, and finishing with what you want together. You'll start to see how your dreams are part of a bigger vision that the universe is holding for you. For example, when I look back at a sample table I filled in, I can see that the universe and I both want me to inspire others through my work. Once you do this exercise, you'll gain confidence and clarity to move forward in your dreams.

Set Your Intention

"Intentions compressed into words
enfold magical powers."

Deepak Chopra, author and New Age guru

Set your intention for what you want to manifest in order to call your dreams in.

You're now aware that you're an active participant in what is showing up in your life. You're constantly creating your reality through your beliefs. Now it's time for you to choose to believe that your dreams are already real. They are in the process of coming true *right* now. Your life is your canvas. It's the greatest expression of your desires.

Your dreams are alive through you.

You are your greatest work of art.

And like all great artists, the creative process of manifesting starts with deciding on what it is you want to create next. The first step is to get clear on what exactly it is that you're calling into your life. You do this by setting your intention.

Setting your intention is simply the process of clarifying what you desire right now. This desire may be different from what you always thought you wanted or it may be a dream you've had for a while, but whatever it is that you desire, it should always feel lighter in your stomach, more exciting than heavy. That's what a clear *yes* feels like. Even if your dream is scary because it's so big, it should still feel exciting. When I work with my clients, I often find they're the ones who are stopping themselves from getting what they want simply because they haven't allowed themselves to imagine that it's possible. They simply haven't allowed themselves to believe that they can do it, so they never set their intention. But you now know that your dreams are possible simply because you have them. So the next step is to set your intention.

How to Apply It

Let's start applying this lesson by writing down your intentions. Even if you've written intentions before, it's always a good idea to write them again, because you're constantly manifesting. And what you wanted before, you may no longer want. Plus, writing intentions over and over again amplifies your faith in them.

So, in your manifestation journal, write down your answers to these questions:

- What do you expect to show up in your life?
- What would you *love* to show up in your life?

Notice if your answers match up. It's okay if they don't yet. You'll get there. Set an intention—something small that you will feel good about, whatever it is, that will happen as a result of reading this book. For example, what would you like to get out of these lessons while you read about manifesting? This will likely feel a little bit more attainable in relationship to where you are now if you're just beginning to explore manifestation.

Now allow yourself to dream bigger than what you are allowing yourself to believe is possible for you right now. You have to open up to your vision in order for it to come into being. If you haven't even imagined it, then you're closing off the doors of possibility for it to ever happen. So write down your two most outrageous intentions for your life. For example, "I am a successful painter exhibiting at the Whitney Museum of American Art. I am married to the love of my life and we travel the world together making art and giving back to communities in need through our charitable organization." Feel good about whatever you write down as your intentions and open up to a new possibility for yourself.

If you're nervous about actually claiming your dream, it's okay. You can never choose the wrong dream. You always have the power of choice. If one thing doesn't work out, you can always choose again. You're never truly stuck in any situation. Remember, the universe is always in motion. Even our cells are constantly moving and vibrating, which means that they are constantly changing. The skin cells in our body are different than they were a week ago or a year ago; everything is always changing. The natural state of the universe is change, so when you fear change, you actually fear the natural state of things. Instead, embrace change, surround yourself with newness, and remember that the things that you are experiencing right now in your life—the people, the circumstances, the surroundings, wherever you are right now, your home, the things that fill your home—those things are what you've allowed yourself to believe are possible for you, up until this moment. And *now*, you have the opportunity to create a *new* possibility. And as I typed this text, the David Bowie song "Changes" came on. See, the universe is speaking through me. It wants you to know that change is good!

So if you allow yourself to believe that other things are possible, then you will experience those results in the people, the circumstances, the situations, the surroundings, and the opportunities that start showing up in your life now. I'm going to help you create that new dream for yourself. And it's okay if it is a different dream than you thought it was going to be. Maybe you always thought you wanted one thing and now you realize, "I don't think I want that anymore." It's okay to change your dream. Listen to your heart. What feels good to you in this moment? What is longing to emerge through you right now?

Plant Your Garden

"Become a possibilitarian. No matter how dark things seem to be or actually are, raise your sights and see possibilities—always see them, for they're always there."

Norman Vincent Peale, minister and author

Be patient and trust that your potential is expanding.

I absolutely love looking at manifestation through the lens of nature. While it's easy to forget, we are a part of nature. The same life cycles that occur within plants also occur inside of us.

Envision the process of planting your own vegetable garden. You plant your seeds, you water them. You put them into the sunlight. You care for them. Every day you nurture your garden. You know without a doubt that your plants are growing. Let's say you've planted potatoes. And the potatoes are starting to grow deep beneath the soil. You can't see them. But you know they're growing. You're excited that they're growing. You don't pull up the potato plant just as it's starting to sprout underground and say, "Why aren't you growing fast enough?"

No, you have faith in the process. You continue to water and nurture your garden. Until one day, your potatoes are finally ready to harvest.

If you had pulled them out too soon, you would have killed your potatoes. You would have upset the natural cycle that was unfolding beneath the surface. If you gave up after only a month of nurturing your plant, you would have never experienced the rewards of the harvest. So many people give up on their dreams too soon. Somewhere along the way, they find "evidence" that they aren't supposed to manifest their dreams. But usually that evidence simply points to an obstacle or a limiting belief. Even through the darkest of winters, plants still emerge and bloom each spring. If you're weathering a storm right now, there is sunshine just on the other side. The sun is still there even if the clouds are hiding it temporarily.

I share the garden analogy because there's a gestation period in manifesting during which you just have to trust. It's completely normal to start freaking out when things don't seem to be happening fast enough. When that happens, remember the garden. Rather than getting frustrated with the lack of evidence around you, imagine that you are supported. Even if you can't see it, know that all is working out in your favor. Trust that you are on the right track.

I love to ask for signs that I'm on the right path. I often see repetitive numbers on the clock or on houses. Some people say those are angel numbers, each with a specific message for you. To me, they are little winks from the universe that I'm headed in the right direction. Some people see pennies, feathers, or reoccurring symbols as signs. Because I'm paying attention, I see them all the time. Celebrate each sign that appears for you. Keep going. Keep the faith. Your focus is what attracts what you desire into your life. So focus on possibility.

You've got this.

Your dreams *are* coming true. It *is* happening. You are *already* living your dream.

Your life is your canvas. It's the greatest expression of your desires. Your dreams are alive through you. They want to be nurtured.

How to Apply It

Like all great gardens, manifesting starts with deciding on what it is you want to harvest next. And once you know what you want to manifest, then you can reverse engineer the process. Start by imagining what you'll feel like once your dreams have fully come to life. If you start from the opposite end—from the finish line, feeding into what it feels like to already have what you desire, it's much easier to trust that you're going to get there.

So let's start with the end result.

Then, once you've thought of what you want to manifest and can feel your desire, ask the universe to show you a sign that you're on the right track. It's truly as simple as that. You can ask out loud, or write it down in your manifestation journal. Then record any signs or synchronicities that show up throughout your day. The more that you pay attention to the things that show up in your life, the more things will appear to support you in manifesting your dreams.

Just like the gardener can imagine the delicious meal from the potatoes she planted, you can imagine what it will feel like to already be living your dream. Trust that your garden is growing.

Advanced Manifesting Tip

Close your eyes and imagine yourself as a tree. Feel your roots going into the earth as you feel the universe effortlessly supporting your dreams. Feel the warmth of the light on your skin and imagine that you're growing and expanding into your full potential. Allow a smile to come to your face. You can continue to meditate here in silence if you want for 5–10 minutes. Allow your thoughts to pass by like a movie, and remain focused on feeling grounded, supported, and expansive.

Expect It

"When you change the way you look at things, the things you look at change."

Wayne Dyer, philosopher, self-help author, and motivational speaker

Expect that your dreams are manifesting.

So you know that manifesting starts with your desire and belief in your vision. But the key element that's missing from many discussions about the manifestation process is expectation. Expectation is so important when it comes to making manifestation easy. You see, Manifestation = Desire + Belief + Expectation. In other words, manifestation is the sum total of your intention, your persistent thoughts, and what you expect will actually show up for you.

When I think about my life, expectation has been a key factor in how I've co-created the amazing situations and circumstances that make me the Queen of Manifestation. I expected them to happen. I have an inner knowing that everything is always going to work out. I actually feel like I'm guided by the universe. I truly believe that I'm blessed, and I always trust without a doubt that everything is working out in my highest good. And because I'm expecting my dreams to unfold, they do.

But if your dreams feel too far off and you don't really have that belief just yet, don't worry. That's where affirmations come in. I'll go into more depth about how to write your own affirmations in Part 2, but for now, know that affirmations are a bridge between where you are now with your beliefs and where you want to go.

They assist you in building up your belief and expectation, and they're a powerful tool for getting you to the place of *knowing* that the things you want are coming to you.

In his book *The Biology of Belief*, Dr. Bruce Lipton explains that biology is based on belief. If you believe you're fat and unhealthy, that's what you become. And the opposite is true. If you truly believe you're strong and healthy, you'll be strong and healthy. Dr. Lipton explains that genes and DNA do not in fact control our biology, but *you* are in control of your life. Recent studies have found that your DNA is actually affected by the energy of your thoughts. Our body is made up of trillions of cells. And each cell has receptors that pick up frequencies shaped by your thoughts and perceptions.

In addition, you're probably familiar with the placebo effect. For example, two different groups of people are given the same pill to heal themselves. But one group's pill doesn't actually have the medicine in it, and the other does. The interesting thing is that after many studies, groups with the fake pill actually heal just as fast. It's because they believe their pills are real. They *expect* to heal.

You see, you can expect good things to happen. You can expect your dreams to manifest.

How to Apply It

In order to expect that good things are happening for you, you need to focus on the good. So take out your manifestation journal and write down the answer to this question: "What's new and good and in my life?" For example, you may write down things like:

- The new client I just got
- The amazing dinner my husband cooked for me last night
- The birthday present that came early
- The trip we just booked abroad

Try to list at least fifteen things, and then keep going. Usually what happens is that when you start writing, you remember other things that might have seemed insignificant before. You start to remember that there are a lot of good things to celebrate. And therefore, you begin to expect more good things to come. I like to do this exercise on a regular basis. You can do it once a week, once a month, or as often as you like. Knowing you're going to do it again brings forth positive expectation of more good things to come.

Advanced Manifesting Tip

When you see friends or relatives, ask them, "What's new and good?" Start to spread the positivity and expectation in the world. You can even do this with your family at the end of each day as a daily reflection practice.

Practice Gratitude

"What you appreciate appreciates."

Lynne Twist, author, cofounder of the Pachamama Alliance, and founder of the Soul of Money Institute

The more you're grateful for what's already in your life, the more things will come to you to be grateful for.

Simply put, the more grateful you are and the more you take the time to appreciate your life, the more life will give you to be grateful for. You've probably heard of this concept before, but have you actually put it into practice?

The positive energy that you put forth when you're grateful helps bring more things into your life to be grateful for. In fact, a recent 3-year study by the University of California found that people who practiced gratitude on a regular basis had stronger immune systems; lower blood pressure; were more positive, happy, and optimistic; and felt connected to a greater universe.

While you can't always control your outer circumstances, you can control your reaction. You get to choose what you focus on in your life. By practicing gratitude, you begin to filter out the negativity and shine a light on all the good things that are occurring. And when you consciously count your blessings, you begin to notice all the good things throughout your life. That's how gratitude expands. It's almost as if your mind has a focus lens that searches out the good and zooms in on it.

If you're in a tough spot right now and you find it hard to name even one thing you're grateful for, remember that even the little things count. Be grateful for:

- The person who held the door for you
- The checkout person who rang up your groceries
- The roof over your head (wherever it may be)
- Having the beautiful opportunity to exist in this lifetime
- Your parents or whoever raised you
- The meal you ate
- The farmers who helped harvest your food
- The breath you just took

When you are able to see how much you're supported right now—even if you don't already have everything you want—you renew your faith in the universe that you're always supported no matter what. And you enhance your ability to manifest your dreams.

How to Apply It

Every night before you go to bed, take out your manifestation journal and write down three things that you're grateful for. This alone will make a huge difference in your life. You might find that you'll want to write down even more things. And that's great! Keep going. Soon you'll have a lot to write about! I tend to write pages of gratitude. Watch your gratitude expand.

Advanced Manifesting Tip

I got this tip from one of my mentors, Peggy McColl. Write down things you want to manifest in your list of gratitudes for the day so that you're grateful for them in advance of them even happening. This way you're using positive expectation in your gratitude practice. It helps you draw in the experiences you crave because you're already feeling grateful for them.

Pay Attention to Your Language

"Language creates reality. Words have power.
Speak always to create joy."

Deepak Chopra, author and New Age guru

The words you speak affect your reality. Use words with intention.

It's easy to get caught up in the negative without even realizing it. But all you have to do to transform your negative mind chatter is to alter your language so that you can consciously create what you want. Be more intentional with the language that you use in relation to your desires.

Pay attention to when your thoughts feel negative. For instance, you have to go to a day job you don't like while you're building your side business. You might be caught saying, "I have to go to work." And that makes you feel dread. Instead of using the words, "I have to," see if you can shift it to "I get to." There's always something good hidden in what you're loathing. You just haven't looked for it. For example, you could say:

- "I get to work with people I love."
- "I get to have an hour-long train ride to work where I get to read a book and listen to my favorite music."
- "I get to decorate my desk with photos of people I love."

So focus on what you *get* to do, not what you *have* to do. Soon you'll start to notice that better opportunities are showing up for you.

Now, there are some situations where switching up your language may feel a little more tricky, but you can find ways to make sure you're still creating joy in your life. For example, a lot of people say things like:

- "I can't afford that."
- "Not now."
- "*When* we have more time we can do it."
- "*When* we have more money we can afford it."

Since we live in a *yes* universe, if you say those things—even just to yourself—you're claiming that you don't have the time or can't afford something. Therefore amazing opportunities will show up, like a fabulous trip, and you won't have enough time or money to go. But that's what you asked for! Things will show up that you literally can't afford. Similarly, if you say "When I have time" or "When we have money," you're putting your dreams on hold for the future. And they will always stay in the future.

It can feel weird to flip the statement and say, "I can afford it," if you really can't. So instead, I recommend saying, "How can I?" That way, you are opening up to possibility instead of closing it off completely. It's like saying, "I'm open to help. Show me the way. I'm willing to seeing how this can happen."

Words are powerful. You might find you continually say certain phrases over and over. One of mine used to be, "I don't have enough time." So can you guess what I kept attracting? More things on my to-do list. If you're constantly telling yourself, "I'm so busy. I don't have enough time," that's exactly what you will be: busy. You won't have time to do the things you love.

How to Apply It

Notice if you have any phrases you continually say that you'd like to flip to the positive and write them down in your manifestation journal. Then cross them out, and write a new phrase that opens up to the possibility of having what you desire. Use the following table as an example to get started.

Negative Phrase	Phrase with Possibility
I don't have enough time.	I am in control of how I spend my time.
I can't afford it.	How can I afford it?
I'm busy.	My life is deliciously full of only the things that I love. I choose how I get to spend my time.

Remember, you are in control of how you feel. And your language is one of the most direct ways to effect a change. Don't feel bad every time you notice a negative phrase come through your language. This exercise is simply about being conscious of the language you're using so that you can choose better feeling words and thoughts.

Part 2

DREAM:
EXPAND THE VISION FOR YOUR LIFE

"If you can dream it, you can do it."
Walt Disney, entrepreneur, animator, and producer

Now that you understand how manifestation works, it's time to expand your dream. Most people don't dream big enough. They stop at a certain point because they think they can only achieve a certain amount of success. But I'd like to take your dream up a few notches and attach it to a bigger mission. Once you do that, you can come back down to where you currently are and then take bigger steps back up to the top. Manifesting this way is a lot easier because you know where you're going and you get there faster.

In this part, you'll learn how to get clear on your vision, which dream to focus on first, a process for dream expansion, and journal exercises to write out your affirmations in the most effective way. You'll also learn how to raise your vibration to match that of the things you desire, how to understand what your dreams and desires mean about you, and how to use visualization.

So if you're ready to expand your dream to allow in even more greatness, read on!

Get Crystal Clear about What You Want

"Your work is to clarify and purify your vision so that the vibration that you are offering can then be answered."

Abraham-Hicks, master universal teacher

Put your order into the universe by first getting clear on what you want.

You can't get what you want if you're not exactly sure what you want in the first place. Let me clarify though, you don't need to know how you're going to get there, you just need to know what you're reaching for. Once you're clear on that, the universe will send you everything you need to manifest your dream!

We all have friends who want to see it first, and then believe it. Have you heard the expression, "I'll believe it when I see it?" That's the opposite of how manifestation works. Those people are thinking they'll recognize what they want when it comes to them. But those are the people who are the most unsatisfied with their lives. They'll never be completely happy because they haven't first taken the time to get clear on what happiness looks like for them. They aren't clear on what they want. You want clarity.

Not sure how to get the clarity you need? Stay with me.

First, close your eyes for a second and imagine that you have all the money and the resources in the entire universe at your disposal. Don't be distracted by your current situation or circumstances. See yourself as totally supported. Ask yourself these questions:

- What would your life look like?
- What would you be doing?

- Where would you be?
- Who would you be with?
- How would it feel to experience this?

There are no wrong answers. Usually the first images or thoughts that start coming to your mind are your intuition—your inner desire—speaking. Allow your imagination to work. Go with it.

From this space, think about that one thing in your life that would make the biggest difference for you if you could actually achieve it. Try to paint a picture of what that is.

Obviously, there is a lot that we want to manifest in our lives, and I get this question a lot: "What thing should I focus on first?" Focus on the *one* thing that's going to make the biggest difference and that will have a ripple effect on everything else. What would that *one* thing be? Once you have that one thing that's going to make the biggest difference and change *everything* for you, I want you to write it down. This is what you are looking to manifest next.

Chances are that big thing that you are looking to create is not the reality of your life right now. In fact, it may feel very far away. And that's okay. I understand. When I was looking for love, I wrote down all the qualities I wanted in my ideal partner. Then when I had recently started dating this guy who I really liked, I wrote down that he was my life partner and the father of our beautiful little girl. Seven years later I found that piece of paper when I was pregnant with our daughter! It had all materialized. Sounds pretty crazy, right? Not at all! Manifestation really works.

How to Apply It

You have to get clear on what you want in order to manifest it. This is the foundation for manifesting your desires. To help you figure out what you really want to bring to reality, try making clarity into a ritual. Boil a pot of tea. Make a cup of coffee or some hot chocolate. Light a candle, sit down with your favorite beverage, and start writing.

Close your eyes and go through the visualization process outlined in the previous section. Think big! Don't let time or where you are now get in the way. The more outrageous, the better! Once you've visualized, write out where you'd like to be in eight areas of your life:

- Home
- Health
- Love
- Friends/community
- Career/creative
- Financial
- Travel
- Spirituality

Now get specific. The universe likes details. Describe where you live. Where is your home? What does it look like? What color is your bedroom and what type of bed do you sleep on? How does it feel living there? What's your view when you wake up in the morning? What do you hear outside your window, and what do you have for breakfast? How much money do you make a year? How much is in your savings account and your wallet, etc. Get the idea? In order to truly feel your dreams, it's best to describe them in as much detail as you can.

And most importantly: *Write in the present tense.* For example, instead of saying "I want to attract my ideal life partner," say "I am happily married to the love of my life." It might feel weird at first, but have fun with it. This is a playful activity. The more fun you have, the more results you will see. Trust me.

If you're still a bit stuck, don't worry. For even more clarity, answer these questions in your manifestation journal:

- **What do you love to do?** They could be small things. But they are clues as to what you really love. That could lead to a bigger vision. For example, I love being outside in nature.
- **What do you want to learn?** For example, I've always wanted to learn how to make a website.
- **Is there a problem in the world that you want to solve?** Think about what it is that upsets you and how you would like to be part of that solution.
- **Listen to your heart.** Is there something that's been speaking to you for a while? Is there a desire that keeps coming back to you but you've been afraid to let it out? Are there dreams, signs, or synchronicities that keep showing up? Listen to the pull that's coming from within, not what other people have been telling you that you should do. They may or may not be a match. That is up to you to decide.

Once you've written out the answers to these questions, use a new page in your journal to list out everything you know that you *don't* want. For example, you know you don't want a certain type of relationship or boss because they didn't work out before. This helps tremendously, because once you know what you don't want, you can create opposite statements for what you *do* want. After you're finished, look at what you wrote for what you don't want and write out the opposite for each statement. Finally, rewrite what you want using the present tense for each statement. Use the following examples to help you along.

What You *Don't* Want	What You *Do* Want	What You Want in the Present Tense
An abusive partner who constantly drains your energy	A supportive, loving partner who energizes you when you're together	I have a supportive, loving partner who energizes me when we're together
A boss who constantly degrades me and questions my abilities	A boss who recognizes my greatness and thanks me for my contribution to the company	I have an amazing boss who recognizes my greatness and thanks me for my contribution to the company
A credit card bill I can't afford to pay each month	A zero balance on my credit card each month	I always pay my bills on time and have a zero balance on my credit card each month
Not enough clients to keep my business afloat	A waiting list of clients who want to work with me	I have a full practice and a waiting list of clients who want to work with me

Congratulations on taking the time to write down your dreams! Doesn't it feel good to allow yourself to imagine what it would feel like if you could have it all?

Advanced Manifesting Tip

Write out your intentions on or around the new moon. The new moon happens once per month, and it's energetically the best time to create a new vision for your life. The new moon serves as a clean slate to dream and set intentions for what you want to manifest next. New moons have also historically been when farmers planted their seeds. The best crops are known to come from seeds planted at the new moon.

Draw Positivity from Your Past

"The past is a rich resource on which we can draw in order to make decisions for the future."

Nelson Mandela, former president of South Africa

Realize that you already are a powerful manifestor by revisiting evidence from your past.

Whenever you're feeling doubtful or discouraged about your big dream, think of all that you've already manifested in your life. I like to call it positive proof from your past, or PPP.

PPP is great for when you're having one of those days when your self-doubt creeps in and you think you should just give up because you've been trying and you're not experiencing results. Even if you're a master manifestor, those self-doubts still appear, but PPP will help those doubts go away.

Think of something fabulous that you've accomplished in your life. It could be something big that you're super proud of. For example:

- Moving out on your own and moving into that apartment
- Applying to school and getting in
- Successfully marketing your business
- Scoring free tickets to your favorite concert, or getting a backstage pass to meet your favorite actor after seeing a play on Broadway
- Experiencing the birth of your child

You did this! It's amazing. You are so powerful. If you could do these fantastic things, you can do anything. It's all about having a great feeling and manifesting from that place.

You have manifested things in your life. There's always something to look back on.

How to Apply It

In your manifestation journal, write down a list of all of the things you've been able to manifest so far in your life. They should be big things that make you light up when you think of them. Do it now, and then refer back to this list when you're having doubts. Think, "Wow, I was able to manifest all of those things!"

That one thing that you're holding onto that seems so big doesn't seem so big anymore because you remember that the self-doubt and fear was there for all of those other things too. But you were able to move through the fear, take action, and manifest. So therefore, you can do anything else.

Advanced Manifesting Tip

Surround yourself with images of your previous manifestations. This could be press, an award, or a picture of you doing something amazing that you manifested. Put up an image of your positive proof from your past in your space or use it as a screen saver on your phone or desktop. It should make you feel good. When you pay respect to the accomplishments that you've already made, you raise your vibration.

Write Your Affirmations

"It's the repetition of affirmations that leads to belief. And once that belief becomes a deep conviction, things begin to happen."

Muhammad Ali, boxing legend

Write out what you want as if you already have it with an "I am" statement.

Earlier in this chapter, you wrote out where you want to be in all areas of your life, and you've gotten specific about your dream.

And now that you've got your dreams down on paper, it's time to write out affirmations based on all you envisioned. What are affirmations? They're short, positive statements that anchor your vision. The shorter the statement, the more powerful it will be. For example:

- I am a successful business owner.
- I own a beautiful white cottage by the beach.
- I have the most amazing, supportive friends.
- I am deeply loved and appreciated for the work that I do.
- Money flows to me like a river.

Affirmations help get you to the place of positive thinking and knowing that things *are* coming to you. By repeating affirmations, you help retrain your brain and reshape your pattern of thinking.

How are affirmations different from what you wrote before? The point is to convince yourself that you already have the things you're trying to manifest. Affirmations can be repeated out loud. But simply writing them down helps you claim your desires. It's taking it a step further than simply setting your intention. You are claiming that you already have what you want. You're doing more than just putting your order into the universe. You're making it real.

Once you've written your affirmations, you can recite them on a regular basis. You can record them, or you can use them to create an affirmation movie (which I'll go over later in this chapter). Even if you simply write your affirmations down and never look at them again, that is enough. It's the act of writing them that sets your dreams in motion.

How to Apply It

Pull out your manifestation journal and open up to the exercise where you wrote down what you wanted in these areas of your life:

- Home
- Health
- Love
- Friends/community
- Career/creative
- Financial
- Travel
- Spirituality

Starting with those visions, write two or three short, succinct affirmations for each category following these guidelines:

- **Use the present tense.** Instead of saying "I will be a millionaire" or "I want to be a millionaire," say "I *am* a millionaire."
- **Use positive statements.** The universe doesn't understand

negatives or "do nots." It only hears the main thought. If there's something you want to avoid, say the opposite in a positive sentence. For instance, if you say "I am debt-free," the universe will only hear *debt*. Instead, say something like "I am financially free." Or instead of saying "I have no back pain," say "My back is strong and healthy." "I want to lose 10 pounds" becomes "My body is healthy and fit. I am a size 6. I feel amazing! I exercise daily. I am conscious of what foods I put into my body, and I feel great about my choices."

- **Be specific.** Instead of saying "I am a successful writer," which could mean many different things, say "My book, *Manifesting Made Easy*, is published. I am a *New York Times* bestselling author! I give talks around the world. I constantly receive letters from readers telling me how much my writing has impacted their lives. I lead writing retreats in Bali twice a year with amazing students." Read those two versions of the same intention aloud and notice the difference that you feel when you read them. The more specific you are, the more you'll be able to actually feel your vision. And that's the goal of writing affirmations.
- **Make it believable.** If you don't actually believe the affirmation, you won't feel good about it and it won't work. So reach high and get excited about the possibilities, but make sure you believe it. Maybe instead of saying you're a millionaire, you're more comfortable saying something like "I make at least $150,000 a year," or "I make six figures a year from my business." While it should be a stretch, it needs to be believable.
- **Add gratitude statements at the end of all of your affirmations.** For example, after the statement "I make six figures a year from my business," you might add, "I am grateful for this bounty of money coming to me from every direction."
- **Include information about how you give back.** For instance, "I use my abilities to make a difference in the world and I feel great about the work that I do."

Once you've done this, add an "I forgive myself" statement to your affirmations. Chances are you're being way too hard on yourself about what's showing up for you. So writing "I forgive myself" releases any negative feelings you have toward yourself from the past. You can also forgive other people in your life. This is especially helpful if there's something you're holding onto that it's time to let go of, like a breakup or job loss. An important thing to note is that when you use forgiveness statements in affirmations, you don't need to state why. If you state the why, your subconscious mind sees the why as an affirmation and you'll focus on attracting more of that to you. So instead of "I forgive you, Michael, for hurting me," you would simply say, "I forgive you, Michael." The same rule applies for yourself.

Advanced Manifesting Tip

Record yourself saying your affirmations and then listen to them regularly. I recorded myself saying wealth affirmations when I was focusing on eliminating my debt. I listened to them daily and was able to free myself from more than $38,000 of debt in less than a year. You can record them on your phone or computer. Make it easy for yourself and have fun with this.

Focus on Your Big Dream

"The future belongs to those who believe
in the beauty of their dreams."

Eleanor Roosevelt, former politician, diplomat, and activist

Begin with the dream that will have the biggest ripple effect on your life.

We talked briefly before about your big dream in the "Set Your Intention" entry in Part 1. It's that one thing that if you could accomplish it, it would make the *biggest* difference in your life. Yes, you're going to manifest *everything* you wrote down, but we want to start with your most important dream and put your energy there first.

Remember, you've already manifested so much in your life. (You did the exercise where you wrote down your past manifestations, right?) This dream should be your biggest vision yet. You're here to create, so make the most of your time here. After all, why not create the best life you can imagine for yourself?

Instead of manifesting any little dream, set the most outrageous intention for your life. Open up to a new dream for yourself.

How do you know you've chosen the right dream? Well, it is *not* . . .

- The thing that will be the easiest to do right now
- The thing that makes the most sense because of the limits you've placed on yourself in your current situation
- The thing that other people around you say you should do or that you think you "should" do

This big dream *is* the thing that lights you up when you talk about it. It is your ideal life. It is something that if you could *do*, *be*, or *have*, you would be on top of the world. It makes you feel lighter. It's so big that you have a hard time even imagining it. You're a little bit scared of how your life would look like if it did come true. But you want it. You want it bad. You've been thinking about it for a while. You're not sure how it's going to happen, but it will. It's got to. Your heart yearns for it. It's the reason you're reading this book.

Got it? Then it's time to take action.

How to Apply It

Once you know what your big dream is, I want you to write it down in your manifestation journal.

This is a safe space, so feel free to expand upon what you wrote before when you set your intention in Part 1. Don't hold back. Get specific. Write it all out. Write in the present tense, as if you already have it. Unlike an affirmation, you're writing more of a paragraph about how it feels to be living your dream. Remember to focus only on your *biggest* dream. The goals you wrote about in all the other areas of your life will support this vision. You don't need to rewrite any of those complementary dreams here though. Just go into more detail on the *one* big thing. You don't need to write a novel. Just get clear on what it is and see what unfolds as you write.

Feeling nervous? Just decide on your biggest dream, and allow yourself to go for it. There is never a wrong decision. You can always decide again once you've manifested your initial dream. New desires will always appear as long as you're alive. That's normal! This is part of what it means to be a master manifestor. All that matters is that you're specific about the description or the feeling behind your dream.

Visualize Your Dream

"You are not given a dream unless you have the capacity to fulfill it."

Jack Canfield, motivational speaker, trainer, and bestselling author

Experience your dream as if it's already happening.

Visualizing is one of the most important tools for manifesting. Experiencing your dream using all your senses shifts your subconscious into believing that your dream has already happened. Doing this will make a *huge* difference in your life!

Visualizing isn't just about sitting in meditation—although that's a wonderful tool—it's really about embodying your dream and feeling it from a vibrational perspective. We visualize because when we feel that vibration of what we want, we attract things to us that are the same vibration. This is the law of attraction in effect. In other words, your goal with visualization is to feel what it feels like to already have what you desire. Doing this attracts what it is that you desire.

Does visualization really work?

Well, I did a visualization session over the phone with a private client, and during our call she envisioned a new book that she hadn't seen before. She even imagined what it would feel like to receive a call from the CEO of the publishing company about her book. Only 9 months later, she got a book deal with that publisher, and the CEO called her exactly as she had envisioned it!

Another private client of mine was working on manifesting a new home. During our visualization session, she really took into account the view from her window. She described it all to me over the phone. Just a few months later, she sent me a picture of the exact view from the new home she had just bought.

I can't make this stuff up!

Sometimes, our dream is something we feel we can't step into because it's so big. For example, a new home, a new car, a dream relationship, or something else we've never experienced. That's okay. Regardless of how far away it might seem, allow yourself to imagine, and step into what it would feel like to have it now.

Test-drive the car you want. Take yourself on an amazing date to a fabulous restaurant. Make space, feel richer in your home, do more self-care. Find something that will make you feel good right now. Visualization is all about allowing yourself to feel the way you want to feel even though you don't yet have that thing or the result that you desire.

How to Apply It

So how do you visualize? Making a vision board and doing affirmations are great steps. But they only scratch the surface of visioning. Use what you wrote in the "Write Your Affirmations" entry in this chapter as your guide in the visioning process.

Begin by stepping into your vision through your heart and experience it through all your senses. Close your eyes and imagine you already have what you desire. Picture yourself at a celebration in your honor. Who's there with you? What are you celebrating? Where are you? What does it look like? Is there food there? What does it smell and taste like? What are people saying to you? What are you doing? How do you feel? Smile and take it all in like a movie playing out in your mind. Enjoy the visualization process. Feel as if you already are living out your dream.

I've created a fifteen-minute visualization that you can download and listen to for free to help you feel your dream through all of your senses—which ignites the manifestation process. It will make your dream bigger than you ever thought possible, and will help your subconscious mind believe you already have what you want. When you visualize your dream as real, you become a magnet for your desires. Get yours here: www.queenofmanifestation.com/freegift.

Advanced Manifesting Tip

In your visualization movie, you layer your written affirmations on top of images that represent them. Then create a slideshow and put it to music that makes you feel good. You can use many different tools on your computer to do this. I like to use iPhoto on a Mac to create a slideshow and then save it as a movie. You can also use www.queenofmanifestation.com/mindmovie/ to create yours with ease. This becomes a film version of what you want to experience in your life. Ideally the video should only be about 5 minutes long so you can watch it every morning. Watching it in the morning motivates you for the day. Stepping into your vision in the morning gets you excited to take action on your dream. And it keeps you focused on what's important. The bigger picture stays in the foreground instead of the background. So, big changes can occur quickly. After just a week of watching mine, I manifested so many of the things in my movie—to the point where it was uncanny how the things that showed up in my life matched the images in my movie. This technique is a must-have for all of you serious manifestors.

Do What You Love

"Let the beauty of what you love be what you do."

Rumi, famous Sufi poet

Do things that make you feel good in order to raise your vibration.

The more you stay in your heart, the easier it is to manifest. What does that mean? Well, when you stay in a happy place, you vibrate at a higher frequency. And that enables you to attract things of a higher frequency. What's the easiest way to make sure that you stay in your heart? Doing things that you love! When you do what you love, you will be irresistibly attractive to the things you want to manifest in your life.

When we look at the reason why we want to manifest something, it's usually because it's going to allow us to *feel* a certain way. So, even if you don't yet have the thing you want, if you can embody the feeling behind it, you can manifest it more quickly.

Ask yourself, "How can I feel that way right now?" You open up to possibility when you ask that question.

Maybe you want to feel happy or free, so you put on some music and dance around. Personally, I like to go on bike rides. That for me is like ultimate freedom. Maybe you want more joy in your life. So you do something that brings you joy. It could be taking your favorite dance class or going to the movies. For each of us, there is something that lights us up and makes us feel really good. Start doing more of the things that light you up, because again, it's going to shift your vibration and help you draw those bigger things that you're looking to manifest into your life. Why? Doing what you love may seem unrelated to your big dream. But everything is connected. If you're happier, you're more likely to manifest what you want. Because in the higher vibration of happiness, you are a vibrational match to your desires. Did you know that Richard Branson's number one intention daily is to have fun? It's no wonder he's one of the richest, most successful business owners, investors, and philanthropists in the world.

If you're having trouble finding what lights you up, go back to your magical child—the source for all your creative energy! As I've watched my daughter grow, I've noticed she smiles countlessly throughout the day. Especially as a baby, everything was a game to her. Tap into the energy of this playful child. Go to that place of magic and joy and see what you discover. What would be fun for you to do right now? If you can't think of anything, I recommend you spend some time in nature. It always raises your vibration. If you do something you love every day, you'll find that the right people and the right circumstances show up to support you. Amazing synchronicities begin to occur, and you can follow your intuition into some great adventures. When you do what you love and live in this energy, you'll begin to see everything in your life as an opportunity!

How to Apply It

Take the time to do something that you love today. That's it! This could be anything, including:

- Going to your favorite yoga class
- Treating yourself to dinner at your favorite restaurant
- Watching your favorite movie
- Riding your bike

- Taking a bubble bath with candles
- Getting a pedicure
- Getting a massage
- Making art
- Making love

It should be something that makes you incredibly happy, fulfilled, and satisfied—no feelings of guilt involved. Just joy.

Advanced Manifesting Tip

Sit down and make a list of everything that you can think of that makes you happy. Whenever you're feeling down, pull out your list and do one of those things to help shift yourself back into a higher vibration.

Notice Synchronicities

"I am open and receptive to all of the good and abundance in the Universe."

Louise Hay, bestselling author of You Can Heal Your Life *and founder of Hay House*

Pay attention to the signs from the universe in order to receive messages to help you manifest.

The universe is always talking to you. The most obvious way to hear the messages is to pay attention to the synchronicities that show up in your life. What's a synchronicity? According to *Oxford Dictionaries*, a synchronicity is "the simultaneous occurrence of events that appear significantly related but have no discernible causal connection." Basically it's a seemingly random coincidence that draws your attention and it almost always leads to a positive outcome if you follow its signs. For example:

- As I was writing my chapter on change being a natural part of the universe, the David Bowie song "Changes" came on the radio. I typed *change* as I heard it.
- I see the word *queen* written on a building sign as I'm walking down the street. Then I see crown hooks in the bathroom of a restaurant I go into. And I'm known as the Queen of Manifestation.
- I'm thinking about getting in touch with a certain friend and then she e-mails me or calls me first the same day.
- At the top of a mountain I hike in India, I run into a friend I made at my yoga teacher's training program.

Synchronicities are full of potential. You might notice small synchronicities in your life or ones that are so huge they literally take your breath away. The more you pay attention to the small synchronicities, the more larger and larger occurrences will appear to show you that you're moving in the right direction. Sometimes the synchronicity is pointing the way to a specific opportunity that requires your action. Sometimes it simply confirms that you're in the vortex of manifestation. The vortex is a term coined by Abraham-Hicks, master teacher of the Law of Attraction, to mean alignment with source energy—the place where all creation begins. Being in the vortex of manifestation means that you're in complete alignment with your desires. They *are* manifesting. Everything is working out just as you intended.

I started noticing synchronicities in my life when I was in college. I remember small things like when I was reading a book and listening to music at the same time, and the sentence I read literally matched the line of the lyrics the band was singing at the exact same time. When I started journaling all the synchronicities that were occurring, I noticed an increase in the occurrences. They made me feel like my life was magical.

When I was in India getting my yoga teacher's training, a few musicians came to our ashram to perform a classical concert. I was so moved, I thanked them afterward and they invited me to a performance a week later. None of my friends from the ashram wanted to go with me, and it was about an hour train ride away. But I really wanted to go, so I went by myself. I didn't have a cell phone, but my friend gave me instructions for how to meet the performers on the stage before the show began. When I got there, the performance turned out to be an outdoor concert that was a part of an international film festival. The musicians from the ashram were performing with their master teacher, one of India's most renowned musicians. And someone had just made a documentary about him that was screening at the film festival. I took the train to go to a concert and when I noticed the synchronicity of the film festival, I decided to stay for three full days. I was invited to dinner at the film festival director's home and it turned out that the directors of the Museum of Modern Art in New York were there too. It was a beautiful synchronicity that I was dining and sharing a car with the directors of one of my favorite art museums, all because I followed my heart—and it led to more opportunities and connections. The musician from the ashram who initially invited me to the concert then invited me to visit his home later in a rural part of India. I ended up taking him up on his offer and it turned out to be the most incredible small art town with artists, writers, and teachers. I stayed with his entire family and I now consider him, his wife, and their kids my Indian family.

Everything is connected. The universe always orchestrates the most magical occurrences if we stay open and pay attention to the synchronicities.

How to Apply It

Take out your manifestation journal and write down the synchronicities that you noticed in your day. The more you pay attention to what's happening around you, the more plugged into the universe you will be, and the easier it will be to manifest. Commit to doing this for a week and you will see a change. Do it for a month and it'll become a habit.

As you go through this book, start to journal all the signs and synchronicities that show up in your life on a daily basis. Do this either at the end of each day, or right after you notice them. The more you pay attention to the positive signs around you, the more you'll notice how supported you truly are by the universe.

Part 3

DARE:
TAKE ACTION ON YOUR DREAMS

"Only those who dare to fail greatly
can ever achieve greatly."
Robert F. Kennedy, former U.S. attorney general

Part of the power of the techniques we've discussed so far is that they get your headspace ready to take the action you need in order to start moving things along. But, as wonderful and helpful as visualization, affirmations, and synchronicities are, you can't just sit around visualizing and saying affirmations all day, waiting for things to show up. You have to take direct action that goes along with your dreams.

If you're not exactly sure about what you can do to make your big dream come true, start small. Let's go back to the restaurant analogy from earlier in the book. Imagine you're at a restaurant. You open up the menu and see your favorite thing on the menu; you want to order it. But the waiter comes and tells you about a new special that sounds amazing. You think about ordering it, but you're a little nervous because you're not sure if it's going to taste as good as what you know you love. Do you play it safe and order the same thing, or do you order the special, trusting that it's going to be delicious?

It's okay if you're the person who orders the same thing over and over again. If you are, you are comfortable with what you're experiencing right now and the results. You might think, "I'm not comfortable. I'm not satisfied with my relationship, or my home, or my job." But you're comfortable in the sense that this is what you've allowed yourself to believe is possible for you up until this moment. And the opportunity for reinvention and bigger dreams is possible *right now*. Getting out of your comfort zone is the only way you're going to experience something new. If you don't take the leap, you play small and you go back to what you're comfortable with because that's all you know. If you want to grow and expand, you need to order the special!

In this part, you'll learn how to take action and you'll realize how delicious the special really is.

Act As If

"Success is more than a desire.
It's a behavior. Act accordingly."
Steve Maraboli, speaker, author, and behavioral science academic

Act as if you are already living your dream to magnetize it.

Hopefully, you've spent some time working with visualization, as described in Part 2. If not, I invite you to return to that section and spend some time visualizing what you desire. If you've done that, it's time to start "acting as if."

When you act as if, you create the environment of the person you're pretending to be. This isn't the same thing as "faking it until you make it." Rather, it's about embodying the feeling of your dream. After all, if you don't believe you can manifest your dream, no one else will!

Even though you might not fully believe it yet on the inside, your outward behavior helps get you there. In other words, your outward actions can assist you in shifting your inner feelings or beliefs. For example, when you're happy, you smile. However, it also works in the reverse. If you smile, you become happy. Smiling first, in order to feel happier, is acting as if.

Think about it. Haven't you ever gotten a new haircut or a new outfit, and then you found yourself acting differently right away? You were probably more confident afterward, right?

Acting as if shifts the way you feel. If you can feel the way you want to feel now, you'll draw in more experiences that help create that feeling.

When I was still in college, I got business cards made that said "Jen Mazer, Artist." At the time I thought, "Who am I to say this? I'm not a working artist." But I did it anyway. And guess what? I started showing my artwork, and people starting referring to me as a great artist! Since then my work has been published in the *New York Times* and featured in *New York* magazine.

I manifested living rent-free in an apartment with a jacuzzi in Manhattan all because I acted as if. I was living on the same block as this magical-looking purple building in the East Village. One day I stopped to talk to a woman who was sweeping outside. She shared with me that she was living there rent-free. I also learned that there was a theater in the building where they put on concerts and plays. I decided right then and there that I wanted to live in that building. So I went to a play in their theater and met the people who were in charge of running the building. I told them I would love to have an apartment there. They said there was an open apartment, but they were reserving it for someone who could build a website for the building. I had never made a website before, but I was taking a computer science class at NYU and I knew I could do it. So I said, "I can make a website." Then I built a sample site for them to see, and they decided to let me have that apartment. I ended up creating that website and living there for ten years. And that was the start to a lucrative freelance career as a website designer—all because I had acted as if. I also unknowingly followed one of Richard Branson's mantras, "If someone offers you an amazing opportunity and you're not sure you can do it, say yes, then learn how to do it later."

Once, while building a website for a musician who was just starting out, I advised my client to put a press link on her site. She felt weird because she didn't have any good press yet. As soon as the site went live with the press link, more and more press started coming in. Just by putting it out there, she manifested it!

Ask yourself what is it that you want to become more of in your life. Declare it. Put it out there, and you'll draw it to you. It's that easy.

If acting as if seems hard, remember that you are worthy. You deserve to have your ideal life. You can be that person *now*. There is nothing stopping you but yourself. So get dressed up and go out. Do things that your dream self would do. Have fun and play the part!

How to Apply It

First think about the big dream you wrote down in your manifestation journal in Part 2. Ask yourself what it is that you want to become more of in your life. For example, do you want to become a successful filmmaker? Now, in order to help you step into that role, I have a fun challenge for you:

Get dressed up as the *dream you* and go someplace where the dream you would hang out. For example, if the dream you has a hot body, you might want to treat yourself to the upscale gym and take one of their classes. They probably have a free trial week. If the dream you is a successful filmmaker, you might go to a film screening at a local film festival. Maybe in your ideal life, you'll be having fine dinners out. So why not enjoy one now? Get dressed up and go to the fanciest restaurant near you. See how it feels to be dining among wealthy people. You might only order a drink, but you'll be in good company. You don't have to spend money to do this exercise. You can simply hang out in another part of town where you imagine yourself living. Or take it a step further and call a real-estate agent to schedule some viewings of dream homes. You could go to a car dealership and test-drive a convertible to see how it feels to drive it around. Those ideas don't cost you a penny, and you can start acting as if you really do have the money to make these choices now. You'll get a sense of what it feels like to be in the space of your dreams. And your body will hold the memory of your experiences. You'll find that doing some of these things for yourself is actually really empowering. Why? Because if you're acting as if, you start to realize that other people around you respond to your vibration and start to see you as the person you intend to be. And that reflection helps encourage your own belief.

Dare to Move Forward with Your Big Dream

"The key is not to prioritize what's on your schedule, but to schedule your priorities."

Stephen Covey, educator, author, and speaker

Flip your to-do list and focus on your big dream first.

Going for your big dreams can be very scary. The unknown can be scary. In fact, all the great things I've achieved in my life have been scary at first, and I think every successful person would say the same thing. But if you take the leap and go for things that resonate with your heart, you will always be pleasantly surprised by the magic that shows up.

For example, my client Michelle tripled her income and quit her steady "gig" to work for herself in less than eight months of private coaching with me. As she puts it, "While working with Jen I was able to build my business to a level that allowed me to quit my job because I learned to be fearless . . . fearless in asking for what I was worth, fearless in how to ask for what I was worth, fearless in presenting what I was worth, and fearless in saying no to things that diminished my worth."

What Michelle did was prioritize her big dream and then go for it. Even though it was a stretch at the time, she decided to invest in renting an office space in Manhattan with the expectation that she would fill her private psychology practice. And she did. Not only did she fill her practice, but she raised her fees and she's now making around $19,000 per month. She's hired an assistant, had a professional decorator redo her office space, and because she's in such a high-vibrational space, she magnetized her soul mate and moved in with him. She's the happiest she's ever been. And it's all because she put her big dream first.

In order to bring your dreams into reality, you need to prioritize them. It's as simple as that. If you continue to put your dream on the back burner, it will always remain there.

Instead, flip your to-do list and put your big dream first. That way there's no avoiding it. You can take small action steps daily to help move your big dream forward.

How to Apply It

Each day in your manifestation journal, make a to-do list for your day that has only three things on it. Those three things are the most significant steps you can take to move your biggest dream forward. Forget about writing things that you can easily check off, like "Do the laundry." Wouldn't you feel better about yourself if you did three things that scared you, but you did them anyway? And afterward you found out that they weren't so scary after all . . .

You could send that e-mail to the person you want to work with. Or call the person you're interested in dating. Perhaps you hire a coach, and finally commit to paying off your debt.

Here's an example: If your dream is running your own successful six-figure business, your priorities might be:

1. Send out my newsletter
2. Make a phone call to a lawyer to set up my LLC
3. Send an e-mail to a potential mentor who's doing what I want to do

These are three little things that will make a huge difference once you get moving. Get into the practice of doing this every morning when you wake up or right before you go to bed the night before, and then follow through!

Get an Accountability Partner

"It's not only what we do, but also what we do not do for which we are accountable."

Molière, playwright and actor

Share your vision with someone who is traveling the same path as you—someone who will not only help keep you on track but also inspire you.

Accountability is a super-important key to easy manifesting. The more you surround yourself with positive and supportive people who are also manifesting, the more you will accomplish.

Right now, you might be having trouble following through on the manifestation assignments in this book. If you're feeling stuck, that is totally normal. Getting an accountability partner will help. An accountability partner is someone with whom you check in on a regular basis to help keep you on the path to manifesting your dreams. Knowing that you have to tell someone whether or not you did what you said you were going to do is one of the greatest motivators. You're way more likely to follow through when you have an accountability partner. If no one other than you knows what you're up to, it's easy to make excuses as to why it didn't get done.

Having an accountability partner not only helps keep you on your toes, but it also creates a space for you to talk specifically and intimately about your goals, your next steps, and anything that's holding you back. If you're hitting roadblocks, your accountability partner is there to listen to you and offer you encouraging support.

Plus, it's always easier to manifest your dreams when you have other people around you who are also up-leveling their thinking.

This partnership can be uncomfortable at first—especially if your partner doesn't follow through on her intentions. If she doesn't follow through, you can ask her, "Why didn't you do it?" Allow her the space to come up with her own answer. Often it's fear that gets in the way. It could be lack of time. Sometimes it turns out that what we thought we needed to do wasn't actually all that important, and something else was. That's fine! You, as the partner, have the opportunity to lovingly hold the other person accountable, not by being mean if your partner doesn't follow through, but by asking her to reflect on it. See if she can still commit to the action and set a new date for when it will be accomplished. Remember though, if you're too easy on each other, it completely defeats the purpose.

You'll find that you and your partner inspire each other to take action, because as one of you begins to take action toward your dreams, the other feels the need to keep up. It's great because it will motivate both of you. You can use your conversations as a space to share success stories and cheer each other on. Each partner's wins propel the other forward. You're also there to offer moral support when you hit stumbling blocks. You might even want to talk more often, or keep an open line for when you're stuck and need help. Once you start talking, you'll figure out a system that works best for you.

How to Apply It

Ask someone to be your accountability partner for manifesting. They could be a family member, a friend, colleague, or classmate. If you need help finding a partner, you can join my free Facebook group at www.facebook.com/groups/manifesteasy and link up with someone else who's reading this book. Then set up your first phone conversation for sometime this week.

When you're on the phone, do these things:

- Introduce yourselves.
- Share what you love and your big dream.
- Decide how you'll hold each other accountable.
- Determine how often you'll talk. I recommend at least once a week and keeping it consistent. So set a regular time and day of the week to call each other.
- Declare what action steps you will have accomplished before you talk again. Then when you check in next, you can hold each other accountable for taking these steps.

It's helpful if you write down both your and your accountability partner's intentions so you have them as a reference for the following week when you check in. You can e-mail your list to your partner as well. Figure out what works best for you two.

Advanced Manifesting Tip

Play the Believing Eyes game that I learned from Sonia Choquette: You and your partner take turns making the other person's dream bigger. Go back and forth as you keep expanding the dream. For example, your accountability partner says, "I want to be a published author." Then you add to the dream by saying, "Your book becomes a *New York Times* bestseller." Then your partner says, "And I get invited to give an interview on TV." Then you say, "And then someone sees you on TV and invites you to collaborate on a project." You keep expanding the dream together based on what the original person wants. You're building the dream together, adding one piece to it at a time.

Create a Daily Practice

"We are what we repeatedly do.
Excellence, therefore, is not an act, but a habit."
Aristotle, ancient Greek philosopher

Manifesting is a daily practice.

All the successful people I know have a daily practice. What's the first thing that you do in the morning? Do you meditate, work out, or make breakfast? Do you set aside time daily for self-care? Have you added in exercise, making healthy meals, and enjoying your favorite activity? What are your working hours? Do you work only four hours a day? If that seems impossible, trust me—it isn't! Working hours are important because you're setting boundaries with the time that you're available. And you'll have greater focus. Most people procrastinate and waste a lot of time. When you limit the amount of time you'll spend on a project or task, you're literally setting the intention that you'll have completed by that time.

Ask yourself, how would you like your day to look from the moment you wake up in the morning until the moment you go to bed?

When creating a daily practice, time management is key. Every day that you wake up presents a new opportunity to be the best you, to experience joy, and to create abundance. After all, you don't manifest what you want. You manifest what you *are*. So if you're happy and taking care of yourself, your vibration will be heightened.

You already have daily habits that are just part of your routine. You can use these habits to help build new practices that will build upon your big dream. Do this by creating new rituals around them. They'll help you stay organized and focused, especially after clearing the clutter. How can you set up a ritualized routine? Well, start by adding a new ritual to a daily or weekly habit that you already have. Adding a *before* or an *after* to what you already do can help make this easy. For example, if you're ritualizing about chores, you can say:

- "After I eat dinner, I do the dishes."
- "After I do my laundry, I put away my clothes."
- "After I take a shower, I put my dirty clothes in the washer."

One of my favorites is "After I walk in the door, I hang my keys on the key hook." It seems simple, but it saves you so much time looking for things when you need them.

You can use these before-and-after statements for your new manifestation practices as well. For example:

- "After I wake up, I meditate."
- "After I meditate, I work out for a half hour."
- "While I eat breakfast, I watch my mind movie."
- "Before I check my e-mail, I post my priorities."
- "Atter I eat dinner, I post my gratitude list."
- "Before I take my lunch break, I take a walk outside."
- The list goes on and on!

These before-and-after statements should be easy to remember. It seems so simple, but the dishes can pile up, or the nicely folded clothes end up sitting on a table for a few days rather than going back to where they belong. If you have rituals, things don't get messy. You stay organized. You get more done. You're happier and free! Setting up a routine that you can follow is so important.

You'll feel better if you make sure that you have time to work out and to do the things that you love while also setting up focused time to work on your big dream. And be absolutely sure to take a break and go outside every day to get some fresh air. If possible, spend some time in nature. This will give you the emotional lift you need so that when you do go back to working on your dream, you'll be even more focused and inspired. Haven't you ever found that when you take a break to go to your favorite yoga class or to run on the track outside, you actually get more work done in less time? It's because these breaks for self-care help increase mental clarity.

Your daily practice should be non-negotiable. Having a daily practice is about making the commitment to yourself to feeling good each and every day. It's easy to get caught up in what you know you have to do as the day goes on. But if you start off your day by feeding your spirit, you'll find you are in a better space to take action. And if obstacles show up to throw you off course, you'll also do a better job of handling them because you've taken care of yourself first. Creating a daily practice is a true form of self-care.

How to Apply It

In your manifestation journal, write out three rituals you can do each day that will help center you and keep you in a high vibrational state for manifesting. Maybe it's meditating first thing in the morning, going for a run, or practicing yoga. It might be journaling your dreams when you wake up. Think of what feels good. Whatever it is for you, write down what daily practices you're going to commit to. Write it out in the present moment as a statement to yourself. For example:

- When I wake up, I meditate before getting out of bed.
- After I brush my teeth, I journal my dreams.
- Then I write my to-do list with only three things on it.

Once you create a daily practice, you'll feel more aligned with what you're manifesting.

Advanced Manifesting Tip

Commit to actually doing your practice for the next 21 days. They say it takes 21 days to form a habit. Once you've done something for 21 days straight, you're more likely to stick to it.

Conquer Your Fear

"When I'm old and dying, I plan to look back on my life and say, 'Wow, that was an adventure,' not, 'Wow, I sure felt safe.'"

Tom Preston-Werner, software developer, inventor, and entrepreneur

Do something that scares you in order to grow.

Your greatest gift lies behind your deepest fear.

If you know that, then why wouldn't you want to do the thing that scares you the most? Instead of looking at what might happen if things go wrong, think about what could happen if things go right!

If you're having a hard time getting over a fear, remember something from your past that you were afraid of doing at first but that ultimately led to a beautiful experience or reward. You must have faith in your ability and know that you are worthy of your dreams. We all come up with reasons why we can't do things. You might think that you don't know enough or that you don't have enough support or money. But those are just excuses.

If you have an excuse, then you don't have to take action and you won't disappoint yourself. If you're someone who often procrastinates, it's most likely because of resistance. You're afraid, so you keep putting off the very thing you know will move your dream forward. Even if you don't know how it's going to happen, all you have to do is ask for help.

The best way to overcome fear is to take action. It doesn't have to be huge action all at once. It can be small steps daily.

I invite you to do that very thing you're afraid of and see how you feel afterward. Your fear could be:

- Sending an e-mail out asking for support
- Picking up the phone to make that call you've been dreading
- Going to that networking event
- Applying for a new job
- Publishing your first blog post
- . . . and many more

Remember not to get stuck on the outcome. The universe might have an even better plan for you than you've imagined. So stay open.

Your action doesn't have to be perfect. If you wait until you know it all, you'll never make a move. Just do what you can. Put yourself out there, and trust that you will learn and grow through the process. You will get better through practice.

What's the worst thing that could happen? Chances are you'll stay in the exact same place you're in now. But on the flip side, what's the best thing that could happen if you take action on your dream? I always envision the best-case scenario. You see, the courage is in the act itself, not in the outcome. It's in being vulnerable and putting yourself out there. Be proud of yourself for doing it in the first place.

I came across this acronym for the word *fear* that I love:

FEAR = false evidence appearing real

As you've gone through this book, you might have found some of the exercises scary. Ask yourself why. For example, if writing your affirmations is scary, it's probably because it makes them real.

It means you're really doing it! Notice what the block is that's inhibiting you from moving forward. What are you afraid will happen if you actually achieve your dreams?

For me, I had a hidden fear of becoming a mom. I always wanted to have a daughter. But when I was in labor, I realized I was most afraid of actually being responsible for another person.

I had been dreaming of this moment. I so wanted a baby girl with the man I love, and it had all manifested. I was full-term and had an easy pregnancy. I envisioned myself having the perfect, easy three-hour labor. It was going to be fabulous! I bought a birthing pool, hired my doula and midwife, and was prepared for a beautiful home birth. But things didn't turn out exactly as I had envisioned them. After twenty hours of labor at home, I still wasn't fully dilated. The pain was so unbearable that I threw up twice. I didn't think I could do it. I was ready to give up. It was at that moment that my friend Angie said to me, "Jen, you can do this. You're ready to be a mom."

And that was it. That's just what I needed to hear to allow my body to fully open up and dilate. I pushed for about twenty to thirty minutes (that was the easy part), and our daughter was born. She had been actively trying to be born as well, just as your dreams want to emerge through you. We were working together!

As much as I had prepared for the birth, I couldn't fully visualize myself as a mom. I wasn't sure that I could do it. Being pregnant was easy. But the thought of actually having a child to care for scared me. It wasn't until I heard my friend's words that I was able to release my hidden fear. We all have these hidden fears. And that fear, I believe, is what made my birth so difficult.

Behind your biggest fear lies your greatest gift.

There's an old saying that if your dreams don't scare you, you're not dreaming big enough. The things that are the scariest are the most rewarding.

So what is it you're afraid of?

How to Apply It

Do something you're afraid of today. This may seem like a simple exercise, but it's a powerful releasing tool that helps you go from being stuck to taking action. Remember, every time you're afraid, visualize things going well. Imagine what you want. Imagine yourself overcoming every obstacle. What does it feel like? Then take the action you need to overcome it.

Focus on your successes, not your failures. If you're still having trouble taking action, remember a time from your past when you did something you were afraid of and it turned out way better than you had imagined. Think of everything you've been able to accomplish in your life because you did take action. The more you can recognize everything as an opportunity, the less you'll be afraid. The universe is here to support you!

Go for the No

"My dad encouraged us to fail growing up. He would ask us what we failed at that week. If we didn't have something, he would be disappointed. It changed my mindset at an early age that failure is not the outcome—failure is not trying. Don't be afraid to fail."

Sara Blakely, founder of Spanx

Stretch yourself and make a big request related to your dream.

I was on the subway once in New York City and the man sitting next to me asked me if he could have the magazine I was reading.

Not just read it, or borrow it, but straight up, "Can I have it?"

I was shocked.

"No, you can't have it. It's my only copy."

But I loved the question.

I loved how he was pushing the envelope to see how far he could take this conversation and how much he could get out of it.

So I said, "But I loved that you asked. How cool!"

Most people don't ask for what they want, especially if it seems like they'll get "no" for an answer.

The man told me he was working on a project in which every day he made requests and was *looking* for rejections. I love this, because if you're not receiving rejections it means you aren't reaching high enough and you won't experience new results.

This man was comfortable receiving "no" for an answer, and you should be too. If you go for the *no* you'll find that you're more comfortable when the time comes for you to step out of your comfort zone to reach for your dream. You won't be so scared to go after a bigger dream when no is a possibility. You see, the courage is in the asking itself. If you know you might receive a *no*, it's not so scary.

Chances are you're playing small. You know there are bigger things inside of you that are longing to emerge. But you might be scared to make the leap—to take bigger risks. Maybe you're scared of rejection, of failure, or of the shame of looking bad. But guess what? Once you aren't afraid of rejection, you can conquer anything, because you're not attached to the outcome.

I continually apply this principle. I once wrote to the head of a major business conference that was more than $5,000 a ticket to attend. I explained who I was, what I stood for, and asked if she would give me a scholarship to go for free. Right after I sent the e-mail, I freaked out. Maybe I shouldn't have sent it? But then I reaffirmed my intention. I wrote down an affirmation that I was attending the conference, put it up in my office, and a day later, I got an e-mail back saying she'd love to sponsor me to attend. I was exactly the kind of person they wanted to be there. I had made an outrageous request. I went for the *no*, but I stayed open to the possibility of a *yes*. The positive outcome of a yes was greater than the fear of a no. And I know from the connections and friendships that were born at that event that I truly was meant to be there.

With manifestation, you have the desire, belief, and expectation that everything is working out in your favor. Therefore, it doesn't matter if you get rejected because you know in the end, it is all working out in your highest good. Who knows what you'll gain when you're not afraid of rejection!

How to Apply It

My challenge for you is to make a big ask and look for the rejection. See what no's you can get . . . because you just might receive a yes. And wouldn't that be fun?

What can you do in the next 24 hours to receive a rejection? Write down your desired outcome of your ask in your manifestation journal in the form of an affirmation.

Have fun with your rejections. See how far you can stretch yourself.

Impress the people you ask with your courage, and see what amazing reactions you receive.

Keep the vision, act as if, then just get out there and ask! You won't ever get anything if you don't ask for it. What's the worst thing that can happen? Someone says no. And then you'll be in the same place that you are right now. You are always fine. You're in the perfect place. By practicing gratitude, you know that you're already fine as you are. Therefore, you don't need to receive a yes. You're unattached. You are manifesting. You are powerful beyond belief. You are worthy. You are loved. Feel good about each ask that you make and each no you receive. It means you're stretching and new things are on their way to you!

Treat Your Dream Like a Business

"Your work is going to fill a large part of your life, and the only way to be truly satisfied is to do what you believe is great work. And the only way to do great work is to love what you do."

Steve Jobs, cofounder of Apple

Take your dream seriously and focus on it daily. Seek out support from others who have already manifested what you desire.

It's time to get serious about your vision. If you want to show the universe that you mean business, then you need to treat your dream like a business. Your dream is no longer on the back burner, something you've been thinking about doing for a while but haven't gotten around to. Now your dream is front and center. It's your mission, your priority.

In order to manifest your dream into reality, you need a team of people and systems supporting you. For example, if your dream is to open up a coffee shop, you want to seek out the advice and support of other coffee shop owners. Find someone to be a mentor who has already accomplished what you're looking to do. If you're feeling lost as to how to move forward on your projects, don't worry! You just need guidance from someone who's already been there and who's done what you want to do. Most successful people follow a model that was given to them by someone who has already been there. So, you want to do the same. Once you understand the basic principles, you can adjust the model and re-create it. But you want to have some knowledge of those who came before you.

I'm sure you know the saying that you first need to know the rules in order to break them. We look to mentors for advice because of their experiences and wealth of knowledge. They can help guide you to be the person you want to be. There's no secret to it. We all need to seek advice from experienced people in our field. It may seem scary to reach out to someone you admire, but won't it feel so good once you have someone you can call or e-mail to ask for help? Wouldn't it be amazing to have some of the people you look up to on your side?

A mentorship doesn't have to be an ongoing relationship. A mentor could simply be someone you speak to on the phone to ask a few questions about how they got started. Your mentoring could even come from a book written by someone who teaches you how to do what you want. Perhaps it's a memoir of someone who's already accomplished what you desire.

Remember what I said about conquering your fear? This is the time. We are all just people having similar life experiences. And we all come from the same source. Approach your mentor as a fellow human being and a friend rather than someone who is better than you. You are amazing! You deserve to be surrounded and supported by other amazing people.

How to Apply It

To start treating your dream like a business, first take a moment to write down in your manifestation journal a list of potential mentors who could help you fulfill your dream. Start with five people you admire. They could even be people who are super famous in their fields. What's important is that they have some knowledge you're looking to acquire. Do some research and see if you can find the contact information for them or their assistants.

If you can't find their contact info, see if they're giving any public talks or have any performances or exhibitions coming up that you can go to.

Next write down another five potential mentors who are more accessible. They could be acquaintances or people who live or work nearby.

Write Some E-Mails

Once you identify these people, take the time to compose a few e-mails telling them how much their work has influenced you, and invite them to coffee or to have a phone conversation to discuss your current dream. Keep the following tips in mind as you compose the e-mails:

- Do your research on the people. It's important to understand who they are and find out a little bit more about their background before you get in touch. This shows that you're genuinely interested in them.
- Give them a compliment. Show them that you really know their work or their life. People love it when you've taken the time to find out more about them and you can convey that you have an understanding of their successes.
- If you know someone they know, make sure to mention it! It will level the playing field, and they'll be more likely to respond.
- Tell them you're looking to do something similar to what they're doing (or have done) and that you'd love to ask them a few questions about how they got there.
- Keep the e-mail short. Busy people don't like to receive long e-mails.
- Make sure to follow up. They might not get back to you the first time.

You'd be surprised at how happy a lot of people will be to talk about their work and answer any questions you might have about how they got there. Who knows, they may even be so interested in what you're working on that they want to help!

Have Questions Prepared

When you get to sit down with your potential mentor (and you will, because you're already working to manifest that meeting), ask her or him the following questions:

- How did you get to where you want to be?
- What steps did you take to get started?
- What was it like the first few years?
- Were there any mistakes that you made that I should avoid?
- What skills do I need to be successful in this field or endeavor (whatever your dream entails)?
- Are there any resources I should be aware of?

Take notes during your conversation. You'll want to use these notes to help you create action steps to prioritize your dream.

Network

If it's a business you're manifesting, write down five industry events that you can go to in the next 3 months to network. Schedule these events in your calendar and make sure to go to at least one per month. When you go:

- **Bring your business cards.** You want people to remember you. This way, the people you meet have a way to get in touch. Even better, ask other people for their cards. This puts you in the power position. That way you get to do the follow-up if you want to.

- **Wear something memorable.** I always like to put on a signature accessory, jacket, or shoes. It should be something you feel good in.
- **Talk to people and make connections.** This is your time to shine. Be authentic. Be inquisitive. Lead with questions. If you ask someone what they do, they'll usually follow up by asking you the same question.

Follow up with the people you meet right away while the memory is still fresh in both of your minds. You can do this by sending quick "Nice to meet you" e-mails refreshing their memories about where you met and what you talked about. If you'd like to continue the conversation, you can ask them to get on the phone, or meet for coffee. Tell them what you loved about your conversation.

Finding a mentor and surrounding yourself with successful people truly lifts you higher. When you're in the presence of greatness, you rise to meet it. This is a surefire way to fast-track the manifestation process.

Advanced Manifesting Tip

Make sure to follow up with people you reach out to but haven't heard back from yet. They might not get back to you the first time you reach out, but this does not mean that they're not interested in helping you. It's not a no unless it's actually a "no." If people don't reply, it's simply because they're prioritizing their own dreams. So send a follow-up e-mail or make a phone call to check in and make sure they received your message.

Build Your Dream Team

"A journey of a thousand miles begins with a small step."

Lao Tzu, philosopher and founder of Taoism

Enlist other people to help you carry out your vision.

Once you have a mentor, it's time to think of the other people you can ask for support so you can focus on manifesting your dream. If you're doing too many things, it's going to be hard to make progress on any one thing. Gay Hendricks, who coined the term *upper-limiting*, says that we should strive to always be in our "zone of genius," which is the area in which your soul shines. If you're good at something, but someone else could easily do it for you, enabling you more time for what you truly love, then it's time to delegate responsibilities and tasks to make your life easier. Similarly, if there are things that you're currently doing that you don't enjoy at all, you'll definitely want to let go of them. For example, I could set up appointments with all my clients myself. But it isn't a task I actually enjoy. So I hired an assistant to help me.

Remember, manifesting is vibrational. So if you're doing tasks that aren't high-vibrational for you, it will be more difficult to stay in a high vibration to manifest. Stay focused on areas that bring you joy.

How to Apply It

Go back to where you wrote down what you want in all the areas of your life in the section "Get Crystal Clear about What

You Want" in Part 2. Think now about who you want to be on your team for each area and write it down. Remember, you're writing down the help you want in your dream life, even if you don't know how it's going to happen now. Here's an example of what this could look like:

- **Home:** cleaning person, personal organizer, personal assistant, babysitter
- **Health/physical:** nutritionist, personal trainer, health coach, private chef
- **Love:** relationship coach
- **Friends and community:** support network of friends, accountability partner
- **Career/creative projects:** business coach, mentor, lawyer, virtual assistant, web developer, brand strategist, PR person, intern
- **Finances:** financial coach, accountant
- **Travel:** travel agent
- **Spirituality:** spiritual mentor

Now prioritize which help would make the biggest impact on your life, allowing you more time or freedom.

If there's something that you don't know how to do, or don't want to learn, hire someone else to do it for you. You can start by asking a friend to help you in one specific area. Or there are a lot of college students who would happily intern for you for free in exchange for real-life experience.

Once you commit to getting help, you'll find the resources that will enable it to happen. When you have a support system in place, you're less distracted by other tasks, and you'll notice that you're able to manifest even more abundance because you have more time to focus on what you love! And when you stay in a place of joy you attract the right people and circumstances to you.

Advanced Manifesting Tip

Create systems for yourself even before you have a team. These systems can be as simple as a how-to for your babysitter, or knowing where to put incoming mail once you've checked your mailbox. Ultimately you are the one who knows which systems are best for you. Take a moment to figure out what in your life feels heavy or takes up too much of your time. Pay attention to areas that feel chaotic or obstacles that keep repeating for you. Those are the areas that need to be systemized. The more systems that you can implement, the more you will accomplish and the more you will manifest what you desire. In your manifestation journal, write down what systems you will create to make your life easier. Then go out and create your first system.

Create Daily Reminders

"It's not selfish to put yourself first. It's self-full."

Iyanla Vanzant, inspirational speaker and spiritual teacher

Surround yourself with things that remind you that your dream is happening.

By now you have a pretty good picture of what your ideal life looks like. And you've had some practice stepping into it.

But obstacles can show up that take you out of a positive space for manifesting. And it can be easy to forget that you are actually in the perfect place right now. While you nurture your garden, you might want to remember what you actually planted! Gardeners often put signs up in their gardens labeling the vegetables they planted with pictures of the final crop. It's not just to stay organized. This way you're less likely to pull up the sprouts before they're fully manifested. And you remember that you've planted seeds, and all you need to do is continue with the manifestation process. There's a gestation period for your dreams, and so it's best to surround yourself with positive reminders of what you're creating.

And if something shows up that pulls you off track and has you doubting that your dreams are coming true, daily reminders help you trust that all is working out in your highest good. They even can train your subconscious mind to tune into the frequency of what you're creating.

How to Apply It

To help you remember to stay focused on your big vision, take the time to set up daily reminders. Here are some fun ideas:

- Change your password for Facebook, your e-mail, or other applications you use daily to mirror one of your affirmations. For example, you can use something like "Imake$350,000," "Iamorganized," or "PublishedAuthor."
- Write out one of your affirmations on a note card and place it on your mirror so that you see it every time you go to the bathroom.
- Pick out an image of your dream life (the house, the family, the awards show, and so on) and put it up on the wall in your home. It may be a single photo. Or you could create a vision board.
- Use one of the images you picked out or a note card with your affirmation on it as the bookmark for the book you're currently reading.
- Set your phone or computer screen saver to be an image of your ideal life.

There are a lot of ways to create daily reminders. Do what feels good for you. There's no right or wrong and you can't have too many reminders. As with everything, you get to choose.

Advanced Manifesting Tip

Pick an object that serves as a reminder of your big dream and carry it with you. This could be anything from a small stone, to a pendant from a necklace, to a shell. It can be anything as long as it has meaning to you and is small enough to put in your pocket, your purse, your wallet, or to wear around your neck or wrist, etc. Then whenever you're feeling doubtful, hold this object and feel good inside, feel supported, and trust that all is unfolding as it should and as you are manifesting right now. The universe has your back!

Schedule Your Dreams

"A dream is just a dream.
A goal is a dream with a plan and a deadline."
Harvey Mackay, businessman and author

Make space in your calendar to plan for your dreams to occur.

Have you ever caught yourself saying, "Someday . . ." or "Yeah, I'll do that later," or "I can't possibly think of doing that now. I have other things to do first."

We have all done this, but you are now consciously manifesting and you're dedicated to making your big dream a reality. So, if you haven't done so already, it's time to schedule your big dream.

What is the point of writing the date on the calendar? Well, small steps add up. And when you set a date on your calendar to make your dream real, the universe starts to take your dream more seriously. This is because on a subconscious level, you expect your dream to manifest on that date. You're also showing the universe that you're creating space for the new dream to emerge. And by putting your dream in your calendar, you're saying no to everything else—thus setting a clear boundary that you're manifesting that or something better.

For example, if you're looking to manifest a dream house, write down when your move-in date is. Write down when you want to sell your current place, etc. If your dream is to run a marathon, write down the date of the race. Once it's scheduled, you'll start doing what you know you can do to make it happen.

I remember that I wanted to go to South Africa for the World Cup when it was held there in 2010. One of my closest friends was performing at the opening ceremonies, and it was a once-in-a-lifetime opportunity to attend. But at the time, I didn't know how I was going to make it happen. I needed to manifest the money for the ticket quickly. So I put the exact dates for the trip in my calendar and blocked off the time. I also added an image advertising the World Cup to my mind movie that I created and visualized myself there daily. And guess what? I manifested the money for my ticket, went to South Africa, and attended the opening ceremonies of the World Cup. Not only that, but I hung out backstage with some of my favorite people and had one of the most incredible experiences of my life.

Now if the date you put in your calendar comes and you haven't manifested your vision yet, it's okay.

One of my best girlfriends wrote down that she would meet her husband on April 1 in the Bahamas. On April 1, she had a date with a guy, but they were in New York at the time. Still, her intuition told her that he was her husband. So instead of being upset that she wasn't in the Bahamas, she asked him to meet her at the local bookstore in the travel section (by the books on the Bahamas). And now, two years later, they're married! This is a perfect example of staying open to your dream even if you aren't exactly where you intended to be at the time, and it ends up turning out better than expected. Even if the date passes and you aren't where you thought you *should* be, chances are you've taken action that's moved you in the direction of your dreams. And something better is on its way to you. You can go with the flow of life and allow any situation to work out in your favor. Not only are you imagining your future, but a part of it is you actually tuning into your psychic side when you write down your dreams in your calendar. Don't second-guess yourself!

How to Apply It

Grab a calendar and schedule the dates for your big dream. I recommend using a free online calendar. They're easy to edit, make it easy to schedule recurring events, and you can schedule things for years to come. Once you've scheduled the big dates, go back and schedule smaller things that you know you can do now to move your dream forward.

To schedule these smaller action steps, work backward from your big-dream dates. You might not know exactly how to make your dream real, but you do know some small things that you can do to get there. For example, if your dream is to run the New York City Marathon on Sunday, November 6, maybe you join the local marathon team on June 5. You run your first fives miles on May 1. Then you might put down that you join the gym on March 6. Work backward from your goal. You get the picture!

Advanced Manifesting Tip

To really make sure you're manifesting your dream, take the scheduling a step further by clearing any other obligations you have during the dates that you've determined. This sends the message that your dream takes priority. Even if your dream seems farfetched, how can you expect it to manifest if you don't treat it like it's real? If you want to take a dream trip to Paris, write down the dates and schedule them. Request time off from work for the week you scheduled your Paris vacation (even if you don't know yet how you're going to manifest the money).

Part 4

DISCOVER:
LEARN WHAT'S BEEN HOLDING YOU BACK FROM YOUR DREAMS

Are you consciously trying to manifest your vision, but you aren't experiencing the results you want? Are you hitting roadblocks? Or maybe you go in cycles. It's feast or famine.

It's common for people to reach a certain level of success and then have obstacles appear out of nowhere. Why does this happen? Well, you're most likely holding onto limiting beliefs that need to be cleared away.

You may not even be aware that you have a limiting belief. But what you do know is that the goal you're chasing isn't progressing, and you just can't figure out why. In this part, you'll discover what's been holding you back and learn how to clear away anything that's standing in the way of manifesting your dream life.

Learn to Deal with Resistance

"Do you press the 'pause' button—the 'until' button in life by saying 'I can't be happy until . . .'? Press the 'play' button and rejoice in the nowness of the moment."

Michael Bernard Beckwith,
founder of Agape International Spiritual Center

Resistance is a natural occurrence and means that you're moving.

You may only see resistance to your dream as a problem. But, in fact, this is totally normal. We all face resistance. And it just shows that you're moving ahead.

You may be familiar with Sir Isaac Newton's third law of motion, which states that every action has an equal and opposite reaction. So when you have forward motion, there's also pull. That's resistance. Imagine that you're floating in a beautiful lake. When you're still, you don't feel much resistance. When you start to swim, you feel resistance, and it's a good thing! It means that you're moving. It's natural, completely normal, and okay. The third law of motion is not just about the physical world. It's a natural law of the universe. Everything has an opposite. There's yin and yang, up and down, positive and negative. You get to choose which perspective to focus on. But the other one is always there.

Whenever you move forward, you can expect some resistance. And now that you know that resistance is natural, you can celebrate it. Resistance just means that you're making progress on your visions! If you expect resistance, then it's not surprising and you can deal with it a lot better. "Oh, hey there, it's you again, Resistance. I know what to do with you."

So now that you know that resistance is perfectly normal and that you can expect it to show up, it's time to ask yourself what you are resisting and why. For example:

- Are you procrastinating when you should be finishing up a project?
- Are you putting off a conversation you need to have because you just don't want to have it?
- Are you avoiding a messy desk?

Resistance usually points to a fear or limiting belief of what will happen if you do or don't accomplish a task. So ask yourself: "What is the result that I would like to achieve? What's the ideal result of taking action?" And "How would doing that thing make me feel?" Remember how to visualize as you learned in Part 1 and feel into the end result. When you can take a moment to tune into how it will feel when you've already manifested the thing you desire, it helps you to take action. For the examples we discussed earlier in this section, you could think:

- I am so grateful I've finished my project. I feel spacious and accomplished.
- I feel so much better now that I've had that conversation. I feel lighter, seen, and heard.
- I love how organized my desk is. I feel organized and empowered.

Author Steven Pressfield talks about the notion of "turning pro," or committing to showing up fully—no matter how much resistance you might feel. Commit to the end result. Commit to yourself and to your dream, because it wants to emerge through you. Consider how having accomplished your dream will make you feel. Show up and make manifesting that dream a daily practice. So often, dealing with resistance is simply a matter of getting started.

For example, when I started writing this book that I'm so excited about, I felt resistance. But once I actually got started and blocked out time to write, the words started flowing. And I thought, "Oh my gosh, it's so much easier than I thought it was going to be. Why was I resisting?"

Recognize that your manifestations are on their way. Have complete faith in the universe, knowing that it's working in your favor and that you have your dreams for a reason. Once you do, you can feel good about resistance.

How to Apply It

If you still have a knotty feeling in your stomach when noticing resistance, it means that you're pushing, pushing, pushing, way too hard. When you're over-efforting, it's a sign that you doubt the universe and you're out of alignment. It's in those moments that I invite you to take a step back. Take a deep breath and say the beautiful affirmation that Louise Hay, author of *You Can Heal Your Life*, created to help release resistance. Simply say, "I'm willing to let go of this need for this pattern of resistance. I trust the universe and I'm in charge of my life."

Then take action today that's in alignment with your vision even if you feel resistance! Know that the universe is always on your side. There's a reason you found your way to this book.

Identify Your Limiting Beliefs

"It is our interpretation of the past, our limiting beliefs, and our undigested pain that stop us from being able to move forward with clear direction."

Debbie Ford, New York Times bestselling author of The Dark Side of the Light Chasers

Your limiting beliefs show up in the form of old patterns and obstacles.

Now that you're clear on your vision, you have the belief systems in place, and you're taking action toward your big dream by prioritizing your life and your daily habits, you are already manifesting! But you may be held back by something that you aren't even aware of: limiting beliefs.

A limiting belief is a well-meaning thought that was there to serve as protection. It protects you from being hurt or feeling pain. It protects you from the unknown. This protection feels good, so it's easy to stay in your comfort zone instead of taking the leap and experiencing something new. Some common limiting beliefs include:

- **I'm not worthy:** You don't think that you actually deserve to manifest or live out your dream due to a multitude of reasons. You don't think you have enough expertise. You compare yourself with other people who are successful and think that you don't deserve as much happiness or success as them. Perhaps as a child your parents shut down some of your dreams and their voices are still playing out in your head.

- **I'm not good enough:** You aren't experienced enough. You didn't get enough training. You always delay taking action on your dreams because you think you need another certification. Or maybe you did something bad in the past so you feel guilty about your dream. Perhaps the job or relationship you're going for is so wonderful, you feel like you're not good enough for it.
- **I'm not supported:** Your partner doesn't understand the law of attraction or doesn't support your dream. Your family thinks you're crazy for going for your dream. You don't have enough help or a team of people supporting you. You think you have to do it all by yourself or wait to ask people to help you until you manifest something else first.
- **I don't have enough time:** We all have the same amount of time in each day. It's simply a matter of prioritizing. Notice if you keep telling yourself, "I don't have enough time." Where have your priorities gone astray? If you keep repeating that phrase, you'll constantly feel overwhelmed.
- **I might fail:** Fear of failure often prevents people from starting in the first place. If you're afraid of failing, I invite you to play out a failure scenario in your head. What would you do if you failed? You'll most likely find that it's not as bad as you thought. You can always make another choice and bring yourself to a better place afterward. Failure is a good thing. It means you went for your dream. And you probably learned from it in the process.
- **I'm afraid of success:** Often a fear of success is a fear of what will have to change when you succeed. Because at a certain level, you're comfortable with what's around you right now. Notice if you think things like: "If I make a lot of money, everyone will be asking me for it." "I'd feel guilty if I made more money than my parents." Remember, change is the natural order of the universe. Instead of focusing on the worst thing that could happen with success, think of the best-case scenario.
- **It's going to be difficult:** More often than not, you're overcomplicating things. You think something is going to be difficult because it was before, or because you witnessed

> it being difficult for someone else in your life. But who says it has to be difficult? When you're in alignment, you'll realize that all the support you need is already there for you. Manifesting is easy!

If you feel these things, it's okay. These thoughts once served a purpose. But in order to break through to the next level of success, you have to understand *your* limiting beliefs and let them go. So don't push your limiting belief away. Instead, welcome it. Thank it for coming in. Be grateful for it because there's a message in it for you. And you need to hear it because it will take you to a new place where you can reach a new level of success, growth, happiness, joy, abundance, and love. If you don't hear that message it's going to stay there and you're not going to be able to let it go. Understanding your limiting beliefs gives you the opportunity to clear what's no longer serving you. You simply need to allow them to come, and then allow them to go.

I really want you to be able to go from this place of doubting if your dream can actually happen to really believing that it totally, without a doubt, *will* happen. You're good enough to make it happen, to experience the things you want to experience in your life.

How to Apply It

In your manifestation journal, finish these sentences:

Life is . . .

I am a(n) ______ person.

Earning money is . . .

I cannot live my big dream because . . .

If I live my big dream . . .

I always . . .

Did you notice anything negative come up? These are beliefs you want to focus on clearing.

Congrats! Identifying your limiting beliefs is *huge*!

Understand the Upper-Limit Problem

"It was very humbling to realize that my worries were there just to make me miserable. It was even more humbling to realize that I was the guy who had his finger firmly pressed on the misery button. It was wonderful, though, to discover that I also had the power to quit pressing the button."

Gay Hendricks, psychologist and author of The Big Leap

End the cycle of self-sabotage and open up to the possibility of even greater happiness.

Most of us have a hidden belief that we can only reach a certain level of success in our lives. It's what we've allowed ourselves to believe is possible for us in terms of business, relationships, and finances. You might think there is only so much love you can have, or only so much money you can bring in. This capacity for how much you can have is your own inner glass ceiling. When you start to bring in more than what you believe is possible for you, you subconsciously block yourself from receiving any more. For example, if you already have a successful relationship, how can you also have a successful career? This sort of self-sabotage is called *upper-limiting*, a term coined by Gay Hendricks, psychologist, *New York Times* bestselling author of *The Big Leap*.

The idea behind upper-limiting—and breaking free—is simple: Your thoughts create your reality. You see, everything in the universe expands. If you focus on the negative, it will expand. But if you can focus on the good, it will expand. For example, if you expect things to be easy, fun, and rewarding, chances are good that they will be. But if you dwell on the negative, are fearful of the future, and expect things to be difficult, that's probably what you'll experience. What do you want to expand in your life? What are you focusing on? Are these two things a match? If not, something needs to change.

Remember, change is our natural state of being. The cells in our body are constantly changing. So if we fear change, we fear our natural state of being. It is safe for you to release these old stories and expand. Simply identify the fear and see how it relates to what's going on in your life. If you've reached your upper limit, it's time to raise the ceiling and allow in even more abundance. Ask yourself this question posed by Hendricks: "Am I willing to feel good and have my life go well *all* the time?" Saying yes is the best thing you can do for yourself. You can experience positive change if you're willing to let go of your old beliefs.

How to Apply It

In your manifestation journal, write down where you feel you're upper-limiting. For example, maybe you're doing the following:

- I'm picking fights with my partner.
- I'm settling for less than what I deserve to make at work.
- I'm choosing to stay in a career I don't love anymore.

Then ask yourself if you're willing to allow even more love and success to come into your life. What would it feel like to have even more good in your life? Begin to imagine it. Then write it down in the present tense in your journal. For example:

- I am willing to have a great relationship with my partner.
- I am willing to get paid what I deserve at work.
- I am willing to take the leap and leave a career I don't

love. I am willing to step into something greater that's a reflection of who I am becoming.

Keep expanding on the positive and see what comes through on the paper.

Advanced Manifesting Tip

Once you've released your old beliefs, create some new ones by creating a mantra. These new beliefs should be the exact opposites of the ones you just let go of, so create a mantra that is directly opposite to the beliefs you released. It might feel weird at first, but that's only a sign that you need the repetition. Here's an example:

"Every day I manifest success as I inspire others around me with my light. I am supported and deserve all the beautiful gifts coming my way. I love myself. Every day, I'm getting better and better. It is easy to make a living doing what I love. I manifest with ease. I am so grateful for the miracles and success I experience daily."

Congrats on breaking through your inner glass ceiling!

Discover Your Old Stories and Patterns

"The thing always happens that you really believe in; and the belief in a thing makes it happen."

Frank Lloyd Wright, architect and interior designer

Rewrite your old stories to move on to something better.

You know that your limiting beliefs come from your past, but now you need to find out exactly where they came from in order to experience a release. Chances are the limiting beliefs you have are deeply rooted. It could be a belief system that's been ingrained in your head since childhood. Sometimes we subconsciously take on beliefs that our parents had. For example:

- You have to work hard to make money.
- It's difficult to raise a family.
- Rich people are self-centered and wasteful.
- It takes a lot of time to get what you want.
- You have to make sacrifices and settle.

The first step is to understand what images and stories you experienced when you grew up. Let's say that when you were little you won an award and your parents told you not to brag about it because it would make your sister jealous. So you kept your successes to yourself the rest of your time in school. That situation might still be playing out in your life today. You apply for a new job with a fantastic salary. But on a subconscious level, that old belief is still playing out. If you get the job, you'll be making more money than your sister. So you sabotage yourself because you want to spare someone else's feelings of jealousy. And you do something on a subconscious level to mess up the interview process. But once you realize this all goes back to the time your parents told you not to make your sister upset, you can begin to notice the ways this pattern is playing out in your life and you can stop it.

When I was growing up, I used to hear, "Money doesn't grow on trees!" I witnessed my father working long hours to provide for us. He often missed family dinner. And I wished we could all be together more. This subconsciously taught me that you had to work hard to make money. Even though we had money, we always shopped for clothes from discount stores. If we did go to a department store, we bought things that were on sale. I realize now that my parents were subconsciously passing on to me a belief that was actually passed down to them from their parents. My grandfather used to own a discount clothing store and, when my mom was little, she only wore clothes from the store. Years later, although she made a lot of money, she still only bought clothes at a discount—even if they were major brands. The idea of paying full price for something seemed outrageous to her. So on a subconscious level, discounting things in order to make them appear more valuable rubbed off on me. When I first started my business, I often discounted my services in order to make them appealing. I thought, "No one will buy this if it's full price. Everyone loves a sale." I had an old pattern of undervaluing my worth. I was grateful when I recognized these old stories because once I understood where they were coming from, I was able to let go of them from a place of love. I am not at all mad at my parents. In fact, they're the most amazing, loving, and supportive parents in the world. But we all carry with us our own patterns that have been passed down to us.

You too have old stories from your childhood that are currently playing out in your life. All of these stories paint a picture of what beliefs might be under the surface, showing up as limiting beliefs that are stopping you from manifesting all that your heart desires. You need to take a moment to explore the past in order to make peace with it and stop the cycle. You can rewrite your limiting beliefs once you know where they came from.

How to Apply It

In your manifestation journal, write down the answers to the following questions:

- What did your parents say or show you about money?
- How did that influence your financial growth today?
- What was your parents' relationship like?
- How did your parents' relationship influence your relationships today?
- What did your parents tell or show you about work?
- How does that impact your life today?

Congrats! Feel good about understanding where your beliefs have come from. From here you can forgive the people involved, including yourself, for holding onto the fears associated with it for so long. But for now, feel good that you recognized the pattern. That alone can help unblock stuck energy.

Replace Your Limiting Beliefs

"Once you replace negative thoughts with positive ones, you'll start having positive results."

Willie Nelson, musician and activist

Allow negative thoughts to come to the surface so that they can leave.

Limiting beliefs will come up throughout your life. But through observation, being open to new information, and being willing to try new things, you can begin to change your perceptions, which will change your reality.

There's a myth that you have to stay positive all the time. It's actually okay when negative thoughts come up. If you pretend that they're not there, what you're really doing is avoiding them. And then they will stay there. But if you can allow them to surface, you can understand your limiting beliefs and let them go.

Behind every obstacle is a beautiful opportunity for growth. So if you're currently hitting roadblocks, it's simply an opportunity to realign with who you truly are. It's a good thing when you notice you're out of alignment. Then you can readjust. When you take the time to allow whatever is bubbling under the surface to reveal itself to you, you'll see there's a great lesson in there that you don't need to keep repeating.

One of my favorite tools to use to acknowledge my negative beliefs and replace them with positive feelings is the Emotional Freedom Technique (EFT). EFT is an easy-to-learn method that can transform and empower you to make the changes you want in a way that will last. EFT is a type of acupressure tapping based on the ancient Chinese meridian system that helps free up the body's energy system to promote physical and emotional well-being.

Acupressure is similar to acupuncture in that it involves stimulation of the body's meridian points, but acupressure utilizes touch instead of needles. The Chinese meridian system is like a highway that runs throughout your body, carrying chi, or energy. All your memories and emotions are stored in your consciousness. If there's a negative memory from the past, it will be stored there, causing a roadblock in the system, until you recognize it and release it. Light pressure on your meridian points through EFT tapping while stating the "problem" can relieve stored emotions so that there's a flow in your system.

First you need to identify what your problem is. It could be that you're angry at your boss, or you feel bad about the weight you've gained. Whatever's bothering you at the moment is a great place to start. EFT has been used to help people eliminate food cravings, quit smoking, overcome pain, get rid of limiting beliefs around abundance, and more! It's an amazing, fast, easy tool that you can use at any time on your own. It only takes a few minutes, and it's been proven to reduce stress, which is of course connected to limited beliefs.

When practicing EFT, you can tap on either side of your body. You don't need to do each side. No matter which side you choose, it will work the same way. You'll use your pointer finger and your middle finger held together to gently tap on each of the points in the following list. You'll also need to come up with a phrase to use in conjunction with the tapping. It always starts with "Even though I . . ." and ends with "I deeply love and accept myself anyway."

The EFT tapping points you'll need to know are as follows. When practicing EFT, be sure to tap the points in this order:

- **The karate chop point:** This is on the side of either hand halfway between the base of your little finger and your wrist. You'll use this point to begin your tapping session while repeating your set-up statement. You'll usually stay at this point longer at the beginning of your tapping session to repeat your set-up phrase three times.
- **Top of the head:** This is the center of the top of your head, where your crown chakra is, the top chakra of the seven chakras of your body, associated with enlightenment.
- **Eyebrow:** This is the inner endpoint of your eyebrow right above your nose.
- **Side of the eye:** This is the inside edge of the bone that's on the outer corner of your eye.
- **Under the eye:** This is the inside edge of the bone right below the center of the eye.
- **Under the nose:** This is the area right in between your nose and your top lip.
- **Chin:** This is the indentation of your chin.
- **Collarbone:** This is the center of your chest. Instead of tapping with your pointer and middle finger as you do with the other points, it works best to curl all of your fingers and gently tap with your entire hand in circles around this area.
- **Under the arm:** This is best described as the point on the side of your body where a woman's bra would fall. It's usually around halfway up your rib cage. You can reach across your body with your hand to tap the opposite side of the body for this point.

Tap each point roughly seven times while saying your phrase before moving on to the next point. You only need to say your phrase once. The tapping is an undercurrent. Think tap, tap, tap, tap, tap, tap, like the seconds on a clock.

How to Apply It

Begin using EFT by using a set-up statement. "Even though I'm feeling ______ I deeply love and accept myself anyway." Then allow yourself to actually state your negative thoughts as you go through each meridian point. Let's use the example of being mad at yourself for the weight you've gained.

Your statement would say, "Even though I'm mad at myself for the weight I've gained, I deeply love and accept myself anyway" or "Even though I'm feeling fat, I deeply love and accept myself anyway." As you can see, there are many ways of doing this. Say your set-up statement three times as you tap on your karate chop point. Then you move through EFT as follows:

- **Head:** Tap the top of your head seven times while saying whatever you're feeling, like, "I'm so fat."
- **Top of the head:** Tap the top of your head lightly seven times while saying, "I always eat too much."
- **Eyebrow:** Tap your eyebrow point lightly seven times while saying, "I feel bloated."
- **Side of the eye:** Tap the side of your eye lightly seven times while saying, "It's so annoying."
- **Under the eye:** Tap under your eye lightly seven times while saying, "I hate when people stare at me."
- **Under the nose:** Tap under your nose lightly seven times while saying, "It makes me feel so insecure."

Then once you've gotten rid of all your negative emotions, reach for the most believable positive statement. And continue tapping through all the points, enhancing the positive statements as you go along.

- **Chin:** Tap your chin point lightly seven times while saying, "But there *are* things I love about myself."

- **Collarbone:** Tap your collarbone lightly in a circular motion while saying, "I'm smart."
- **Under the arm:** Tap and say, "I'm a good dancer."
- **Top of the head:** Tap and say, "I love the way dancing makes me feel in my body."
- **Eyebrow:** Tap and say, "I'm grateful for my body."
- **Side of the eye:** Tap and say, "It allows me to move."
- **Under the eye:** Tap and say, "I choose to feel good in my body."
- **Under the nose:** Tap and say, "I love myself."
- **Chin:** Tap and say, "I love my body."

You'll notice that as you keep tapping on each point, more positive thoughts will flood in to support your beliefs. You can continue to move throughout the tapping points in this order until you feel at peace. Remember that you can use EFT tapping any time you want to clear a limiting belief that shows up.

Realize What You're Tolerating

"You teach people how to treat you by what you allow, what you stop, and what you reinforce."

Tony Gaskins, motivational speaker, author, and life coach

Notice what is out of alignment in your life and adjust the sails.

Your outer world is a reflection of your inner world and what you tolerate is a mirror of what you believe you deserve. You could be tolerating a bad relationship, a messy home, an outdated computer, or a difficult client. The list of what you're tolerating might not be the most fun thing to look at, but the outcome of confronting it can be so rewarding. After all, it's difficult to manifest what you truly want if things you don't want surround you.

You see, physical clutter actually clogs your mental space. There's a reason that the personal organization market is booming. Have you ever found yourself procrastinating on a project by cleaning your space? It's because you actually think more clearly without the clutter. But once you've cleared the physical clutter (which we'll get into in Part 5: Detach: "Make Room for the New"), emotional clutter often takes its place.

If you're tolerating a bad relationship and you know deep down that you need to have a difficult conversation—but you keep delaying it—it will keep repeating in your mind over and over again until the situation is handled. And if that thought is on repeat, there's no room for your positive affirmations for what you're manifesting.

First, get rid of any unfinished projects that are weighing you down. Either finish them or decide to move on and eliminate them from your list. The same goes with organizing your finances. If you haven't opened a credit card bill in months because you're too scared to see how much you owe, how do you ever expect to get a handle on your finances and pay off that debt? Trust me, I was there.

I had gotten myself into more than $38,000 of debt and didn't even realize it because I didn't ever keep track of my bills and expenses. So for me, it all started with finally coming to terms with what I owed. I sat down, listed out each balance on each card, and hired a money coach to get me started. And once I did that, I was debt-free in less than a year! All moving forward took was facing my fears and taking charge of my situation. Your situation might not be related to money. It may be a relationship or lack of self-care. Only you know what you're tolerating. What aren't you completely satisfied with in this moment?

How to Apply It

In your manifestation journal, make two columns. On the left side, write a list of all the things you're tolerating. On the right side, leave space for action steps. After you write your list, think of what action step you can take for each item in order to address it. For example, your chart may look like this:

What Are You Tolerating?	What Action Steps Can You Take?
Credit card debt	Make an appointment with a financial advisor, take time to organize your finances, or have a conversation with your spouse about money
Messy house	Hire a cleaning person
No time for self-care with my kids constantly wanting my attention	Hire a babysitter
Tasks that I hate doing at work	Get a free intern or hire a virtual assistant to help out

Getting help with the things that bog you down the most will make you feel lighter, and you'll have more time to focus on what you love—which will help you manifest your desires. Write down everything that's on your mind. Your manifestation journal is yours alone.

Advanced Manifesting Tip

In your manifestation journal, write a list of all the things that are currently on your to-do list for the day (as we discussed in the "Dare to Move Forward with Your Big Dream" entry in Part 3). If you haven't yet created yours for the day, do it now. But this time, allow yourself to list everything that's on your plate, not just your top three priorities. Then go through the list and see if all the things on your plate still resonate with you. For example, if there's a project that you no longer want to be a part of and you're not committed to doing it, you can choose to let it go. Start crossing off things that are no longer in alignment with who you are and where you want to go. You can either delegate these items if you've committed to them, or simply take them off your list altogether. Then circle the things that give you the most excitement. Those are the areas you'll want to focus on first. It's okay if there's a dream that you had for a while that no longer resonates with you. It simply means there's a new dream that wants to emerge at this time. Trust this process and your inner knowing.

Meditate

"Silence is a source of great strength."
Lao Tzu, philosopher and founder of Taoism

Take time each day to quiet your mind.

Meditation is the act of spending time in quiet thought, usually while seated. Having a daily meditation practice is fundamental to staying calm, connecting to your source, and manifesting the life of your dreams. It's an opportunity to literally clear your mind of your to-do list and focus only on your breath and the present moment. When you do, you'll feel calmer and more at peace. Not only will you start to crave these quiet moments to yourself, but as you practice, you'll increasingly notice a heightened awareness in your intuition.

Remember that everything is energy. We attract things that are of the same vibration as what we are radiating. Think of a radio. You turn the dial to tune into a specific station. If you're on AM, but you want to be on FM, you won't find what you're looking for. And if you're at 88.8 FM, but you want to listen to 89.3 FM, all you will hear is fuzz. It's only once you can tune into that specific frequency that you start to hear the music. It's the same thing in life. You must match that specific vibration in order to manifest it. For example, say you want to attract $100,000 a year. You need to act as if you already are an abundant person who earns at least $100,000 a year. If you come from a place of lack and can only conceive of making $60,000 a year, you won't be able to bring in the money that you desire. So how would $100,000 feel? It's not about spending money like someone who makes that much if you literally don't have it; rather, it is about feeling into that specific vibration of abundance. Abundance is at a higher frequency than lack.

Meditation is an easy tool to get you to a higher vibration. It's really the art of relaxing your body and quieting your mind, which allows you to break negative mental patterns and habits and allow space for higher wisdom to come in. You see, there's information out there, but you might not be attuned to it. If you learn how to clear your mind and tune into the right channel, you'll notice your intuition speaking to you more and more. You'll feel more connected to the universe. You'll start to make better decisions that are coming from a place of positivity and love rather than fear and questioning. This is why I always recommend that you pay attention to any synchronicities occurring in your life. These are signs from the universe. Make a habit of journaling these things when they happen.

It can be tough to find the time to meditate, but you have to make it a priority. You only need fifteen minutes to get it done. So turn off the TV, and let go of the need to check social media or get on your phone. By making time to practice, you honor the fact that you're a spiritual being having a human experience. You make the time for yourself to connect to the universe and to raise your personal vibration. The time you spend meditating is your personal time to recharge, let go of worry, doubts, or fears, and just be present in the moment. If you take time for self-care, you'll find that you're even more efficient in all the other areas of your life. The more you care for yourself, the easier it is to manifest, because you're feeling good. And it's in that feeling-good place that you attract more things to you that also feel good. Meditation might seem complex, but in fact it's quite simple.

How to Apply It

To apply this lesson you first need to learn how to meditate. Meditation doesn't need to be overwhelming. It can literally be as simple as sitting in silence for a few minutes. Start small and you can expand your practice. Here's how:

Choose a Time

To start, pick a time of day when you can meditate regularly. You might want to meditate at 5 A.M. before the kids wake up, or 9 P.M. after they go to sleep. It might be at 3 P.M. or during your lunch break. Pick a time that works for you that you can easily stick with.

Choose a Quiet Place

Find a quiet place where you can sit without any distractions. Try to go to the same place daily to practice. Eventually, just by stepping into that space, your mind will feel at ease. While you're in this place, turn off your cell phone and any other devices likely to make noise while you meditate.

If you want to, you can put on music (something classical or spiritual). With time, you'll find you don't need music to go into a state of meditation.

Relax and Get Comfortable

Sit in a comfortable seated position. If you want to sit on the floor, sit with your legs crossed and your spine straight. Roll your shoulders up and back. You can also sit on a chair with your feet uncrossed and planted firmly on the ground. Don't lie down to meditate. You'll only fall asleep!

You can sit with your hands on each knee, palms facing up. Or you can put one hand on top of the other in your lap, also palms facing up.

Focus

Close your eyes. Focus on your breath, inhaling and exhaling. You can inhale to a count of four and exhale to a count of four a few times to get you into a good space. Pay attention to your breath, and as thoughts enter your mind (as they will!) just watch them go by like a movie, and go back to your breath.

You can use your imagination to focus on an area of your mind, such as your "third eye," the point between your eyebrows, just above your nose. The third eye is traditionally used in Indian culture as a focal point because it enhances your intuition. Imagine a white light there. Other areas of focus are your heart chakra (literally, imagine focusing on your heart) and the top of your head (or your crown chakra). You can imagine a white light coming in through these points, filling your body on each inhale and expanding outward throughout your whole body on each exhale.

If you want to, you can add an image to that point of concentration, like a heart, a deity, a blue diamond, etc.

If you'd like, you can add a mantra (i.e., say something quietly to yourself on each inhale and exhale). Adding a mantra can increase your ability to focus in meditation. It's not necessarily something you speak out loud, but your inner voice hears it. There are many traditional Sanskrit mantras, such as "sat" on the inhale and "hum" on the exhale. "Sat, hum" opens up channels of inspiration. I love using this one when visioning. Each has its own meaning. But you can make up your own. For example:

- Inhale "peace" and exhale "love."
- Inhale "wealth" and exhale "harmony."
- Inhale "ohm" and exhale "shanti." (This one is great for calling in peace.)

Having a mantra just focuses your attention and helps eliminate other distractions. It's a great way to begin a meditation. As you go, you'll find that you'll let go of the mantra and just stay in a state of bliss, breathing in and out.

Be Still

Just sit there. If you're new to meditation, it might seem difficult just to sit still for 5 minutes. You'll notice the ache in your back, or the fly in the room. But try for at least 5 minutes at first.

Like anything, meditation takes practice. The more you do it, the more comfortable you will be. Keep in mind that quieting the mind can feel different for each person. The ultimate goal traditionally is *samadhi*, or enlightenment and peace. It's an individual practice and everyone will have their own experience. You might feel a swirling sensation. You might feel nothing. You might have a vision. All is okay. Don't expect a mind-altering experience. It's more a state of stillness, calm, and rejuvenation. Be patient. Staying consistent in your practice is the key to success.

Put It Into Practice

If you'd like more advanced meditation techniques and guided manifestation meditations, visit www.queenofmanifestation.com to download yours. For now, just pick a time every day that you will sit and meditate for at least 5 minutes. Start with 5 minutes and slowly increase to 15 minutes over the next few days. Then congratulate yourself on your new habits! Look how far you've already come.

Transform Your Negative Thoughts

"A pessimist sees the difficulty in every opportunity. An optimist sees the possibility in every difficulty."

Winston Churchill, former prime minister of the United Kingdom

Behind every obstacle is an opportunity for growth.

You've forgiven. You've named your limiting beliefs and started the journey of transforming them through EFT. But if you still find yourself feeling doubtful or having trouble manifesting at times, it's okay. First recognize when you're having a negative moment and transform that negative into a positive.

Even though you've added a lot of positive thoughts into your head through your affirmations, visuals, gratitude, and positive actions, you can still get caught up in the negative. After all, for most of your life you've been conditioned to think in terms of the negative. It started by being taught the word *no* as a baby. So every time you catch yourself in the negative zone, try to pivot yourself back into the positive. Focus on what makes you feel good—on what you *want* to attract, not what you don't want or think you can't have. Staying positive is a choice. Each present moment provides the opportunity to do so. You create your reality. Positive conditioning is a practice, so don't get frustrated when a negative thought pops up. Just try to shift it away. Soon more and more positive thoughts will replace the old patterns of negativity.

For example, the next time you catch yourself saying, "I can't stand my boss," you can rephrase it to "I *can* stand my boss, even if I don't like her behavior." Better yet, find an opposite statement about your boss that is likeable. For example, "My boss really loves her family." Just by shifting it to something positive—even if it seems unrelated—you're rewiring your body and changing the vibration that you're giving out. You can also rephrase thoughts. For example:

- Change "I can't believe I missed that train" to "I get to sit and finish reading my book."
- Change "I wish I could go on that trip" to "I'm so grateful I get to spend time at home alone to recharge."
- Change "I have so much work to do" to "I'm so lucky I have a thriving business and get paid well."
- Change "I can't believe my child is having a meltdown" to "I'm so lucky I get to experience being a parent."
- Change "I *have* to" to "I *get* to."

Another way to transform your negative thoughts into positive ones is to choose a sacred grounding object that will remind you that your dream is on its way. It's an object you can infuse meaning onto, like a piece of jewelry or a stone. Hold it and envision your big dream manifested. Then you can carry it with you to serve as a reminder that you're on the right path. Whenever you hear other's doubts and fears, or feel your own limiting beliefs coming up, hold your object and come back to that centered place of calm and knowing. You should always carry your object with you to serve as the anchor for your dreams. It brings you back any time you feel doubtful, scared to take action, or are met with obstacles from the outside world. Feel the object and remember that all is well—that the universe is supporting you, and you *can* manifest your dream.

How to Apply It

In your manifestation journal, write down a thought you would like to reframe. Then come up with new sentences that support the evidence of what you desire. These should be new sentences that make you feel better.

Use the examples below:

- "I have to . . ." becomes "I get to . . ."
- "'I wish I had . . ." becomes "I'm so grateful that . . ."
- "I can't . . ." becomes "I am open to . . ."

Advanced Manifesting Tip

Choose a sacred grounding object to serve as a reminder that your dream is manifesting. Once you have your object, hold it and envision your dream manifested. Once you've infused it with positive energy, choose to either carry it with you or place it in a special spot at home.

Part 5

DETACH:
LEARN TO LET GO OF YOUR DREAM IN ORDER FOR IT TO COME TO YOU

In this part, you'll learn how to detach from an outcome. Here we'll build on the ideas that we've discussed in the earlier parts by turning obstacles into opportunities for growth, letting go of the people and things that no longer are a vibrational match to where you're headed, and making space for your desires. In loosening your hold on your dreams and the things you think you need to be happy, those very same things start to appear. This happens because you're happy now and by detaching from your need for proof, you can truly manifest with ease.

Make Room for the New

"The place we live should be for the person we are becoming now—not for the person we have been in the past."

Marie Kondo, bestselling author of
The Life-Changing Magic of Tidying Up

Organize your physical space to create mental space.

As you learned in the "Realize What You're Tolerating" entry in Part 4, you need to clear your physical space in order to allow manifestation to happen. Your surroundings are a reflection of what's going on in your head, so if your place is a mess, how can you expect yourself to think and act clearly? If someone has a messy physical space, their mental space will be messy as well and vice versa. The universe loves order. What you have in your physical space is merely a reflection of what you've allowed yourself to believe is possible for you up until this moment. So right now is an opportunity to clean house and dream bigger.

Think about what you want to manifest next. For example:

- If it's a soul mate you're after, clean your bedroom.
- If it's a work project, it's especially important to clear your desk.
- If it's better health, make space in your kitchen to sit down and have wholesome meals.
- If it's abundance, splurge on fresh flowers for your home once a week.

Haven't you ever found yourself procrastinating by cleaning before working on a big project? This isn't procrastination at all. You have to clean your space in order to focus. You see, the universe rewards actions. Every time I organize the papers on my desk and file things, I get an e-mail or a phone call from a potential client. I can't explain how this works, but it never fails. It really is that easy.

The universe loves order. So, as organizational guru and author Marie Kondo says, everything should have a purpose and a place. Are there any piles of paper or clothes lying around your space? Even the tiniest bit of clutter disrupts the flow of energy in your home. This clutter could even be hidden, but out of sight doesn't always mean out of mind. Do you have a drawer that you stuff everything into? Go through that drawer. Do you throw things under your bed? Clean it out!

If we keep hiding our messes, it means we're not paying attention to them. But they're still there, and they will prevent us from moving forward. Those hidden spaces or things you throw underneath other things are like subconscious blocks preventing your progress. You want your outer world to be a reflection of your inner world. You want your space to be high-vibrational, just like you.

How to Apply It

Take some time to clean up your space. Organize and file paperwork. Throw out, recycle, or donate things that no longer serve you and bring you joy. Transform your space into a sanctuary that is completely warm and welcoming and makes you happy when you're inside it.

When your space and your mind are clear, you've made room for your new dream to come in.

Fall in Love with Your Wardrobe

"By making room for the new you, you will create a vacuum that the new you will rush in to fill and you will be on your way to the top."

Edward W. Smith, author of Sixty Seconds to Success

Choose to wear things that make you feel good and reflect your dream self.

You did awesome work clearing out your clutter in the previous entry. Now it's time to take it a step further and make sure what you're keeping in your wardrobe ties into your manifestation goals.

Think about what you're trying to manifest right now. Who is the person you want to be in the world? What does that person look like? What sort of style does this person have? What clothes does this person wear? Now look at your wardrobe. Is it a match? For example:

- Is your dream to own your own successful business, but you only hang out in sweatpants and T-shirts? If so, pare down the casual wear, and choose to dress up while you work from home.
- If you want to get fit, but you don't have any workout clothes you feel good in, buy some new ones.
- If you want to attract wealth, make sure you have clothing that makes you feel like a million bucks. Donate the things that make you feel insecure. Those might be clothes with holes or rips in them.

Remember, clothing is all about how you feel when you put it on. And it doesn't have to stop at your clothes. Look at your accessories, purses, and outerwear. Choose items that make you feel like the person you want to become.

The more you can step into your ideal you, the better you will feel—and that shifts your vibration, which helps you manifest.

How to Apply It

Apply this idea by curating your wardrobe to reflect the future self you want to become. First, go through your closet and create two piles. One is for things you will keep (your future self), the other is for things you will donate (your old self). Anything you are no longer in love with or that you haven't worn in over a year goes into the donate pile. Keep only the things that make you feel good. The law of attraction works with your wardrobe. Dress for success. Emulate who you want to be in the world! If you look like her, chances are you'll feel like her and *embody* the person you want to become. You'll be vibrating at the same frequency of your dreams and that will help you magnetize them.

Once you have your donate pile, create a giveaway bag. Then you could host or attend a swap party where your friends bring their giveaway clothes as well, and you can trade. Your old-self items may just be someone else's treasured new wardrobe! After you swap, you can designate someone to take the extra items to a local donation center or thrift store. You'll be practicing another tool for manifesting: giving!

Learn the Art of the Sacred No

"'No' is a complete sentence."

Anne Lamott, author

By saying "no," you create space for a clearer "yes."

In Part 3 you learned how to deal with a "no" response and found that accepting rejection can move you closer to manifesting your dream. Here, we'll take this one step further and you'll learn how to empower yourself by saying "no" and sticking to your guns.

Saying no is a wonderful thing. By doing this, you're setting clear boundaries with the universe. You're saying, "No thank you. I trust that something better, something even more aligned with my vision, is on its way to me." You refuse to settle for less than what you deserve. And you deserve to have everything that your heart desires simply because you desire it.

One of the ways you can say no is to finish old projects that are weighing you down. As you make your priority list each day, are there things that are keeping you stuck? For example, you want to start a new line of business, but you still have old clients you're obligated to work for. And they don't bring you joy. Finish those projects and make space for the new business dream that wants to emerge. Maybe you told yourself you would fix that broken piece of furniture. But the piece is sitting there staring you in the face. Take the time to fix it today. Otherwise, throw it out. If you haven't done it by now, how important is it to you? Once you say no to the things you don't want to do by clearing them from your plate, you create more space to prioritize your dream. You might be unsure about how to make your big dream come true. Remember, start small. Get clear on what you want, and the universe will provide the how through synchronicities.

By saying no to things in your life that don't feel good and aren't in alignment with who you are becoming, you allow more room for what you truly desire to come in. Often we're scared of letting go of a situation because we don't trust that another one is on its way, but there is always another opportunity right around the corner.

When I was in college, I waited tables at a fancy vegan restaurant in New York City. It was my sole source of income and I relied on it. I was grateful for my experience there, but when I was about to graduate from university, I had an inner knowing that it was time to move on . . . but I was afraid of letting the job go. However, I had just graduated with a degree in art and that passion was calling me. If I allowed myself to stay in a job that wasn't in alignment with where I was going, I wouldn't have space for the new dream to emerge. So I gave my notice at work and that same day, I had someone approach me to do design work for them. I had manifested my first paying art gig. It was amazing to me to recognize that as soon as I let go, the universe provided me with exactly what I wanted. This experience has happened to me over and over again in countless situations, and it can happen for you too!

How to Apply It

First you need to get clear on everything that's currently on your plate. Then you can decide which things to say no to.

- **Add everything that's on your mind to your to-do list.** Now look at your list. Things that are aligned with your mission will make you feel lighter. Things that aren't aligned with your purpose will always make you feel heavier. Notice how you feel when you read your list over.
- **Are there things on your list that you can delegate?** Like hiring an intern or an assistant, a cleaning person, a

babysitter, or a handyman. Can your partner take on one of these tasks? Saying no to things that clutter up your life allows your dream to emerge.

- **Figure out which one task you will delegate now to make your life much easier.** Write down who you're going to hire or who you can ask for help. Now go ask for it!
- **Go back and cross off the things that are no longer in alignment with who you are and where you want to go in life.** Remember that you are "acting as if" now (see Part 3).
- **Ask yourself, "Do I feel good when I look at this item?"** If you get a knot in your stomach or if there's something that's been on your plate for years and you keep procrastinating on it, perhaps it's time to cross it off your plate.
- **Ask yourself, "Am I procrastinating because I don't want to do it or is it just because I'm afraid?"** If it's out of fear, leave it on there! Taking one small step a day actually helps to remove the fear. If you're procrastinating because that item just doesn't align with your big dream and your purpose, cross it off. It's time to let it go.

Once you've finished crossing everything off, take a deep breath in through your nose, and exhale loudly out of your mouth, saying "ahhhh." Feels good, right? The more you can clear things off your list, the more you'll open up space to let in new, more exciting opportunities.

Advanced Manifesting Tip

You will continue to get offers for new opportunities. As people ask you to help them with *their* projects, ask yourself, "Do I really want to spend my time doing this? Does it serve my greater purpose?" Get in the habit of putting yourself and your dream first. Other people will always want your help. Every time you open up your e-mail inbox there is a chance you will be confronted with someone else's mission, but you get to decide when and how much you want to give of yourself. Maybe you're on your way to starting a charitable foundation and having someone else run it. But in order to do that, you first must build your own empire. Make a decision from your heart and say no to the things that aren't in alignment with your higher self.

Learn Forgiveness

"It's one of the greatest gifts you can give yourself, to forgive. Forgive everybody."

Maya Angelou, poet and author

As you forgive, you liberate yourself from your past and free up space for your dream to unfold.

Forgiveness is essential to clearing the blocks to abundance in your life. Are you holding onto someone or something that no longer serves you—a negative thought, a painful memory? Take a look at your life and at those around you. Have you been holding onto something that is causing you pain? Dig deep. Is there a grudge that you can't let go of? Every time you think of a certain person, do you feel a knot in your stomach and get upset?

Can't find anyone to forgive? It doesn't have to be someone else—it could be you! Maybe you did something a long time ago that you haven't let go of. Maybe you have a physical ailment that you blame yourself for. Whether you need to forgive a person or thing, this type of negative vibration prevents you from moving forward and manifesting your dreams (even if the person is no longer in your life). It's time to release old hurts and forgive.

This is a huge step and should not be overlooked. You have to clear any blocks you might have before you can allow abundance in any area into your life. Once you figure out who or what it is that needs forgiveness, you're ready to move on.

But how do you forgive? You can't just call up a person that you're holding a grudge against and tell her that you forgive her. That person may no longer be with us, or may no longer be in your life.

Forgiveness isn't about letting others know that you forgive them. In terms of manifesting, what's most important is that you know you've let this particular situation go. And forgiveness is an exercise you'll come back to over and over again. Once you think you're finished forgiving, a new opportunity will arise to forgive again. If you've been particularly hard on yourself for something that happened in the past, it's important that you forgive yourself as well.

How to Apply It

First, step into your heart and see the spirit of who you're forgiving: see why she did what she did, and come from a place of understanding. If you're forgiving yourself, go to a child version of you. It's easier to let go from there.

Most things happen out of fear. So try to see that fear so you can sympathize with the person who hurt you. Connect your spirit to the spirit of the person you're forgiving. Forgiveness comes from a place of love. Close your eyes and tell yourself out loud what it is you've learned, and that you forgive the other person and it's time to release it and move on. Take some deep breaths and release on every exhale. You may have multiple people to forgive. If so, I recommend doing the following exercise for each person.

Advanced Manifesting Tip

Make forgiveness a ritual. First light a candle. Then pull out a piece of paper and write a letter to the person or circumstance that hurt you. Write:

Dear ______,

I forgive you for __________. Thank you for teaching me ______________.

I now release you and send you love.

____

Burn the paper when you're finished. Release it to the ethers. You are now free to accept new, bolder experiences. You've created more space for abundance to flow freely into your life. Congratulations!

Use Ho'oponopono to Ask for Forgiveness

"Forgiveness is the experience of peacefulness in the present moment. Forgiveness does not change the past, but it changes the present."

Frederic Luskin, Ph.D.,
director of the Stanford University Forgiveness Projects

Heal yourself and the world through this ancient technique where you ask the universe for forgiveness.

You can ask the universe for forgiveness and can use this technique to gain forgiveness for yourself and others. To do this, you need to learn an ancient Hawaiian clearing prayer called Ho'oponopono, which says:

I love you. I'm sorry. Please forgive me. Thank you.

You can use this prayer to heal old guilt that you've been carrying around by finally taking ownership of your life.

We now know that everything that shows up in our lives appears because we attracted it to us with our energy and vibration. By taking responsibility for what you've attracted to yourself, you can assuage any guilt that you feel for what you've brought in. It's time to replace blame, anger, resentment, and ego with the understanding that you have the power to change the things that show up in your life. It's a blessing and an opportunity to replace old attitudes and thought patterns with new ones. How exciting!

Let's break down Ho'oponopono and understand why and how it works:

I love you has great healing power. The very act of thinking loving thoughts tunes your mind to that frequency with remarkable and immediate results. The more we can come from that place of love when dealing with others and ourselves, the happier and more fulfilled we will be.

I'm sorry opens the door for atonement by you taking responsibility for what you've brought into your life so far. This meditation can also be used for remote healing—so it doesn't necessarily have to be for yourself. You can say Ho'oponopono for universal peace. Don't dwell on the apology. Just saying it is enough and presents the opportunity for healing.

Please forgive me is about asking forgiveness for forgetting that the universe is Love. We are all unconditional love, and love is truly the key to manifestation. By becoming love and tapping into source energy, we heal, we create, we manifest!

Thank you is simply your acknowledgment that your petition has been heard and is being acted upon. By you taking responsibility for the situations in your life and acting upon them, you are guaranteed a response.

That's it. Say this prayer whenever you're upset—or when you notice others upset around you. You can use this prayer to heal all sorts of situations. For example, if you see two strangers about to get into a fight on the street, or a situation on the news that's upsetting you, rather than turn away from it, or get angry, say Ho'oponopono and direct it toward that situation. I offer you this gift today. Treat yourself well. Enjoy each moment. Forgive yourself. You are doing your best. Give yourself love.

How to Apply It

Focus on what's bothering you right now. Then repeat Ho'oponopono out loud ten times: I love you. I'm sorry. Please forgive me. Thank you. Imagine being filled with white light and then release it out into the universe. You've just sent out positive energy to the universe and to the thing that you want to change and transform. Notice how you feel afterward. Use this as often as you want daily.

Learn to Deal with Disappointment

"Nothing is impossible.
The word itself says, 'I'm Possible.'"
Audrey Hepburn, actress

There is greatness on the other side of disappointment.

No matter how great of a planner you are, how well you write out your intentions, and how much action you take toward your dreams, there's something that's sure to happen in your life . . . and that's disappointment.

You could have gone for a great job interview only to find out they gave the position to someone else.

Or you were in what you thought was a really great relationship, and then your partner totally let you down.

Maybe you had a client drop the ball on a payment.

Or your kids didn't do what you expected of them.

You're disappointed. And it's okay. Disappointment happens. It's a part of the manifesting process and the most successful people in the world actually plan for disappointment.

Why would they do that?

Because if you never stretch outside of your comfort zone, you won't experience anything new. You'll stay stagnant. And staying stagnant never helped anyone manifest the life that they want to live.

Stretching yourself instead means that you're bound to get a few rejections, or to be disappointed in an outcome. It's simply part of the equation. But if you reframe it in the right way, those disappointments can lead you to new heights.

Let's face it, not everything may go according to how you envisioned it, but you can overcome disappointment in the most positive way—one that leads to something even better than what you could have imagined before it. So if you've been feeling stuck lately, or someonc let you down recently—whether it be a client, a friend, a coworker, or a loved one—pay close attention. We all deal with disappointment in our lives, even the best planner or manifestor—it happens to everyone. Instead of dwelling on your disappointment and allowing it to hold you hostage, you need to have tools at the ready that will allow you to flip the situation around into a positive space faster than you could do on your own. Then you can get back to doing what you are here to do—manifest and be happy.

How to Apply It

When you feel disappointment, there's a simple process you can use to help you get back into a positive headspace and continue manifesting.

Feel Good

The first step you need to take to turn your disappointment into something positive is to feel good that you've actually gone for your dream in the first place. The courage is in the act itself. If feeling good in a tough situation seems difficult, remember that the way you feel doesn't need to be dependent on anyone else's opinion, or the way that the situation played out. Whether it's disappointment in a relationship or a job you applied for and got rejected from, it's okay. Feel good that you went for it. The most successful people in the world plan for disappointment. They plan for failure. They're not manifesting failure, but they're not afraid of it either. They know that disappointment is part of the equation. It happens. Successful people learn from their mistakes and move on. You don't have to be upset and disappointed for long.

Be Grateful

Once you feel good, the next step is to practice gratitude in the moment. So when you first receive that disappointment, ask yourself, "What am I grateful for in my current situation? What around me is still good?" This type of thinking helps you put the situation in perspective. In addition, the daily gratitude practice that you learned in Part 1 should already be helping you stay in a positive mindset when that disappointment comes. You can say to yourself:

- "Okay, this didn't work out, but this thing in my life is still good."
- "I'm thankful for . . ."
- "I still have my health."
- "I have a loving partner."
- . . . or whatever is still good around you!

What you focus on expands, so focus on gratitude. That will help shift your vibration back into positivity and attract more things into your life.

Identify an Opportunity

Next, ask yourself, "What is the opportunity in this situation?" Every obstacle has an opportunity. If you've just received a no, it simply means that something else is a clear yes. Maybe the disappointment will lead to you recognizing where you've been out of alignment and learning what you can let go of. Perhaps because this one thing didn't work out, you now see a new avenue that you didn't see before. Disappointment is an opportunity for you to get better and improve upon your life.

To receive the lesson, ask yourself, "What can I do to tweak this process so that it can go better the next time?" It's not about getting even; it's about getting happy. What can you do right now to shift your vibration and stay present? I always recommend doing something that you love, such as:

- Putting on music and dancing
- Going to a yoga class
- Taking a walk outside
- Calling a friend for support

Do something—anything—that will make you happy and shift your vibration. What you decide to do does not have to be related at all to the thing that you are disappointed about. You just have to do something that makes you happy. And, once you get happy, it's hard to stay in that place of disappointment.

Recommit

Look at the lessons you learned through your disappointing experience and then recommit to the vision you're manifesting for yourself. Just because you were disappointed and things didn't go the way that you planned doesn't mean that your dream isn't meant to be. This disappointment simply gives you an opportunity to recommit to your manifestation goal. Recommit to your vision, and stay true to what is important to you. You're on the right track. You've got this. Manifesting is easy. You wouldn't have the dreams that you have if it wasn't possible for you to actually manifest them.

Transform Jealousy

"The flower does not think about competing with the flower next to it. It just blooms."

Zen Shin Buddhist saying

When you recognize the success in others, it means that success is meant for you too.

We've all experienced the green-eyed monster at different points in our lives. You notice something good happening for someone around you and you get jealous. This feeling is part of the human condition.

With social media today, jealousy is something we experience more often than we would like to admit to ourselves. Everyone posts the best parts of their lives online. You see photos online of someone's seemingly perfect house, family, job, and life, and that's when you really start to become jealous and you wonder why your life doesn't measure up. That's really when you start to become jealous of your peers, friends, or even family members, and what they're accomplishing in their lives. Jealousy doesn't feel good, but it can actually be a *good* thing. You can actually take this feeling, pivot it, and transform it into a positive experience that you don't have to be afraid of or feel bad about.

To pivot your jealousy, notice when the feelings of jealousy first arrive. Then, instead of automatically feeling bad because you don't have what your friends have, flip those feelings. Feel good because you now realize that what your friend has is something that you want too. Even if you don't want the exact same thing that you see your friend celebrating, take a closer look and realize that there's something about it that you want to achieve for yourself. Recognize it. You can even say to yourself, "Oh my goodness, I realize I want that, too! Okay."

Once you recognize that your jealousy is caused by something you want, you can actually feel good, because that dream is calling you. The fact that you noticed it in the first place means that it's something that wants to emerge through you too. Otherwise you wouldn't have paid it any mind. Take this realization and start to feel good knowing this thing is actually meant for you.

So feel good that you've magnetized this person who has had this experience or has accomplished this thing into your life. You're the same as she is! Even if you're not in the same room as her, the fact that you're in the same circle, or the fact that you're noticing her achievements, means that you are vibrating at that same frequency. It means that *you* have the power to manifest her success in your own way. It's calling to you, which means that great things are destined for you too.

Many years ago, I had a crush on a guy who I used to see around town a lot. We were friendly and always stopped to talk. Then one day I saw him with a woman. As usual, we said hello and he introduced me to his wife. I was jealous. I had no idea he was with someone, let alone married. Then a few weeks later I ran into his wife by herself. We were both eating at the same restaurant at individual tables. Rather than letting the feelings of jealousy well up inside of me, I recognized that we were the same. I said hello and we started talking. I moved to her table and we ate lunch together. As it turned out, my intuition was right. We had so much in common, and now she is one of my best friends. We've traveled the world together and our kids are friends. We've supported each other through many of life's transitions and I'm so grateful to have her in my life. She's a true soul sister. Any time

I notice that I'm jealous of someone else, I recall that situation. Like attracts like. You are vibrating at the same frequency. There is something there for you if you recognize it.

How to Apply It

Recount a situation or person that made you feel jealous. Is there anyone in your life you're jealous of right now? When feelings of jealousy arise, use this exercise to dissolve them. In your manifestation journal, write out your feelings.

- What are you jealous of?
- Own what it is you really want.
- Write out a gratitude statement for your desire.
- Realize that you've magnetized this person to you because you also are vibrating at the same high frequency. Write out a gratitude statement for being in the same high vibration. Love yourself up.
- Recognize that greatness is there for you too. You have something unique to offer to the world. Write down the ways in which you are special.
- Open up to something greater coming your way that is uniquely suited for you. Write down an affirmation that begins with, "I am open to receive . . ."

Surround Yourself with Positive People

"Great minds discuss ideas; average minds discuss events; small minds discuss people."

Eleanor Roosevelt, former politician, diplomat, and activist

Choose to spend time with people and activities that raise your vibration.

There's a saying that you're the sum of the eight people with whom you spend the most time. Take a mental note of the people you surround yourself with the most. What do you talk about when you get together? Do you talk about what you're working on and support one another's projects? Or do you talk about other people and speak negatively about your circumstances?

If you're complaining with your friends, you're draining your energy. Complaining and gossiping is of a low vibration. When you do those things you're saying to the universe that you're not in charge. You don't have control over your life and how you feel. And that's not true. Instead, spend your time lifting others up. Reflect possibilities and show the universe that you love being in a high-vibrational space. When you are with people who are more advanced than you are, you raise your vibration to meet them there. But when you're with people who drain your energy, you lower your vibration to their level. Wouldn't you rather spend more time with people who raise your vibration? Remember, the higher the vibration, the easier it is to manifest.

It's important to realize who you're spending time with because it's time to get rid of the negative people in your life. You don't need to literally cut them off. Bad idea. Be mindful of other people's feelings. I mean, choose your time wisely and try to spend *more* time with the people you most admire, the people who are doing or accomplishing things with their life, the people who are happy, positive, and supportive of your dreams and desires. Start saying "no" to your friends who are draining, negative, or drag you down emotionally.

Along with that, start saying "no" to things or activities that you don't like doing. You have the power to choose who you want to spend your time with and how you want to spend it, and it's time to start spending that time with people who can bring a positive vibration into your life and strengthen your positive vibration as well.

How to Apply It

Eliminate the negative people and activities weighing you down. If you're feeling overwhelmed, you're not alone. The next time someone asks you to do something with them, check in with yourself first. Is it something you really want to do? Or do you feel you should do it out of obligation? Make a decision from your heart. You don't have to do anything that doesn't feel good to you. Start spending more time with people who lift you up and support your dreams.

Advanced Manifesting Tip

Join a mastermind, a group of like-minded people who are manifesting their dreams. You could start your own mastermind with friends or join a professional mastermind with a coach. Choose to get together either in person or via phone on a regular basis to talk about your dreams and give each other the support and guidance you deserve. You could meet once a week, once a month, or choose to check in daily on group text. Be a mirror to each other's desires. If you want to join a community of people manifesting their visions, join our Facebook group at www.facebook.com/groups/manifesteasy/.

Let Go

"We must be willing to let go of the life we've planned, so as to have the life that is waiting for us."

Joseph Campbell, mythologist, writer, and lecturer

You don't need your dreams to manifest when you're happy in the present and can detach yourself from the outcome.

Throughout the book, you've been doing great work on visioning, releasing blocks, and taking action toward your dream. You're doing your best to hold onto feeling as if you already have what you desire, and you're acting as if. Now it's time to let go of the outcome. Trust that the universe has heard your prayer, and be open to the many different ways that your dream may show up for you. You're not letting go of your dream. You're only letting go of the idea that it needs to look a certain way. But the universe often has better plans than we can imagine for ourselves alone. And in letting go, you're trusting that the universe is your guide. Your intentions have been heard and the universe has your highest good in mind as it says yes to your desires.

If I reflect on how I've been able to accomplish so much in my life, it's all been about positive thinking. I always trusted that the things I wanted in my life would eventually manifest. There was no doubt in my mind that these things wouldn't happen. I truly believed deep down in my heart that everything I imagined was real.

Once you declare what you want and take steps toward your dream, the universe always has your back. Therefore you don't need to be attached to your dreams. You're feeling good in the moment, knowing that everything is unfolding exactly as it should. Non-attachment is letting go of the outcome. Think of it this way: The universe might have even bigger plans for you than the ones you have for yourself.

So why limit yourself to a specific outcome when it could be something that looks slightly different, but works even better for you? Stay focused on your vision, but know that all is perfect with you right now. You don't need anything from the universe but the love you have in your heart.

When I finally let go of the guy I was trying to get to commit to me, he came around. And now we have a beautiful child together. Haven't you ever experienced something like that? Maybe when you break up with someone and start dating someone new, your ex calls. It's because you're doing well in your life and others can sense that. Listen, you don't have to break up with your dreams to practice this. Just don't "need" your dreams. Know that you are beautiful and happy and perfect just the way you are. Being desperate gives off the wrong energy for attraction. Remember to stay present. If you can experience joy in each moment, more joy will come in.

When you are radiant, your energy field expands and you attract the right people and the right circumstances. Just stay open to the synchronicities and signs around you, and you'll be led in the right direction. The more you meditate, the more clarity and peace you'll feel in your daily life. Trust that you are manifesting now. And then release the attachment. You are, and will always be, all right. No matter what religious beliefs you may hold, know that you are a spiritual light being just having a physical experience right now. You are always light—and the more you can remember that, the more you can see it in others, and the more you allow it to shine.

How to Apply It

Remember, if you can experience joy in each moment, more joy will come in. This means letting go of attachment and expectation that your dream has to look or feel a certain way in order for you to be happy. Instead, celebrate what brings you joy right now.

In your manifestation journal, write down a list of everything that makes you happy right now. Start with, "I am happy that . . ." and continue to free write for at least 5 minutes.

Your journal could include phrases like:

- I'm happy that I have alone time while my kids are at school.
- I'm happy that I have money in my bank account.
- I'm happy that I fit into my skinny jeans.
- I'm happy that I found a penny on the street today.
- I'm happy that I heard my favorite song on the radio.

The more you can stay in a happy place now, the more things will come into your life that make you happy.

Advanced Manifesting Tip

Sit in meditation. Close your eyes and imagine that the universe is supporting you right now as you let go of your expectations. As you breathe in, imagine a white light coming down from the universe into the crown of your head and into your heart. As you breathe out, imagine the light flowing into all of the parts of your body, filling you up. Breathe in and allow more white light to flow into the crown of your head and into your heart. Breathe out and allow the light to relax your entire body. Breathe in white light from the universe. Breathe out and feel the love radiating from your heart chakra, expanding your aura. Breathe in white light. Breathe out and imagine the light emanating into your surroundings. Breathe in white light and breathe out; feel the light radiating out into the world. Breathe in and imagine a circle of light flowing back to you from the universe. As you breathe out, you complete the circle of support around you.

Transform Criticism

"Criticism is information that will help you grow."

Hendrie Weisinger, world-renowned psychologist and author

There's a beautiful opportunity for growth in receiving criticism.

We all have an inner critic that's fed from the outer world. And when you receive criticism from other people, you might take a step backward and start to criticize yourself for not manifesting your dreams yet. Fortunately, you can take that inner criticism and change it to positivity to make sure you stay on the path to manifesting your dreams.

We have all have received criticism at different points in our lives and it doesn't feel good. The negativity that initially comes along with criticism can be tough to take and that's when you start to go into a downward spiral. In order to start getting out of this negative place, all you need to do is smile and breathe. It seems so simple, but when you receive criticism, just say, "Okay, deep breath." Just like that. This opens you up to a receiving place and it helps you get out of the place of defensiveness. A receiving place is when you're open to the positive vibrations that the universe is sending to you. You're able to accept the goodness that is being sent your way. On the opposite side, when you're defensive, you're closed off to all of the goodness from the universe. You're not able to recognize or acknowledge it.

After you take a deep breath and move to a more receiving place, you'll be able to ask questions and go deeper into *why* the person who's criticized you said what he said. Criticism can come in the form of rejection or in the form of an actual critique. What is it that this person actually means by her criticism? Is she coming from a place of hurt and blame, or is it actually helpful? This is going to help you determine whether it's deconstructive criticism or constructive criticism.

If the criticism is deconstructive, the person criticizing is usually putting you down so he can feel better about himself. Fortunately, you have the choice not to listen to deconstructive criticism. You can re-evaluate who you decide to listen to, and who you decide to share your big dream with. You might decide you don't want to share it with certain people. Instead, share it with those who are going to be positive and supportive.

If the criticism is constructive, there's learning in it. With constructive criticism, the person is intending for you to move forward in your life. It's supposed to help you learn. If this is the case, notice if there's something that you can improve upon. This is a beautiful opportunity for growth and learning.

Once you open yourself up to criticism, you can be thankful that the criticism was given in the first place. You can be grateful for it because it gives you an opportunity to improve upon something in your life that was out of alignment and that you may not have noticed if you hadn't received the criticism. Now you have an opportunity to improve, grow, and manifest. If you look at the most successful people around you, they're always accepting criticism, tweaking things, and taking new action. They're always using criticism to improve. And we all want to improve and learn in our lives.

How to Apply It

First determine if your criticism is constructive or deconstructive. If it's constructive, open up, and allow yourself to receive.

Ask yourself these questions:

- What is this criticism teaching me?
- What can I learn from this?
- What can I improve upon?

This may be challenging but remember to approach the questions from a place of receiving, not defensiveness. There is always an area where you can do better. You simply need to admit it to yourself.

Release Anxiety

"Happiness is the highest form of health."

Dalai Lama, Buddhist monk and spiritual leader of Tibet

Let go of anxiety and trust that you're co-creating with the universe in perfect timing.

If you've been working toward a specific goal, but find yourself getting anxious when you think about it, you're not trusting that it's happening. Instead, you're nervous that your goal might not happen—and if you're doing this, then that's where your focus is. If you let anxiety over realizing your dream overwhelm you, you'll end up manifesting what you *don't* want instead of what you *do*. This is an easy trap to fall into, but fortunately you can release anxiety while you're manifesting.

First, you want to consider why you're feeling anxious about what you're creating. Where is that feeling coming from? And what would happen if you actually did not manifest what you are trying to manifest? As we discussed in the "Let Go" entry in this part, it's helpful to not be too attached to the outcome when you're manifesting.

If you're feeling anxious about manifesting your dream, there's obviously desire there, but you're afraid of not manifesting it. And you don't want to amplify your fears as you take the right action. Once you've done the work of really setting the intention, it's best to just let it go and come into a place where you trust that your dream is manifesting and you're able to allow yourself to be okay with whatever comes out of that manifestation. Realize that even if you aren't able to manifest your dream, you'll be fine, too. You're actually already fine. Remember that you're always in the perfect place at the perfect time. The universe is showing you exactly what you need at this very moment. And it's providing for you, giving you exactly what you need at *this* very moment.

So to get rid of that anxiety and come to a place of trust, say, "I trust in the universe. I know I'm in exactly the right place at the right time and the universe is working in my favor."

Recognize that you're co-creating with the universe and that all is fine as it is right now. The best practice is to first allow yourself to imagine what would happen if your dream did *not* manifest. Be okay with that, because if you're truly okay with it not happening, then you can release it and you can continue to just do the work. And at that moment—when you let go of the outcome—what you've been working toward will manifest itself.

If you're anxious, that anxiety is coming from a place of desperation. You don't want to manifest from a place of needing it to happen. That's not the right energy to put out. When you need it to happen, it's almost like repellant. Think about dating someone who is really after you. He keeps calling and texting. You can sense his desperation. It's a turnoff, right? It's that same kind of feeling with the universe. You don't want to go overboard: "I need it, I need it . . ." Yes, you're going to do whatever it takes, but you don't *need* it. You are fine where you are right now. Instead, come from a place of abundance and knowing that you have enough. You're perfect just the way you are, even if you don't have that one thing. And if it comes to you, great! That's what I set my intention for, but I don't need it, because I am in the perfect place right now and I trust in the universe.

How to Apply It

Come up with an affirmation that uses the word *trust*. For example, you could say something like:

- I trust that all is working out in my highest good.
- I trust that the universe has my best interest in mind.
- I trust that my dreams are being manifested right now.
- I trust that spirit is guiding me.
- I trust that I'm on the right path.

Once you've come up with an affirmation that you feel comfortable with, use it as a mantra to get you back into that place of knowing that all is working out in your highest favor. Remember, affirmations are guideposts helping us feel the way we'd like to feel. So recite your trust affirmation when you want to instill a greater feeling of trust with the universe.

The Positive Side of Receiving a No

"It is impossible to live without failing at something, unless you live so cautiously that you might as well not have lived at all—in which case you fail by default."

J.K. Rowling, author of the Harry Potter series

Receiving a "no" simply means there's an even better "yes" on its way to you.

Earlier in the book you learned that by going for the no, you can open up to a greater yes, and in the section "Learn the Art of the Sacred No," you created more space for the right yes to come in. Here, I'll share with you the power of a positive no, which is so important because a positive no can actually lead to a yes.

Don't let a no stop you from accomplishing what you want in your life. Instead, look at how that no leads you to a new possibility or a new path that you would not have discovered had you not received that no in the first place. Often, this new path is even better than the original path you were trying to follow.

One time I had a flight that was supposed to go from New York City to California. When I got to the airport, I was told it was canceled and that I was not going to be able to get another flight that night and I'd have to leave in the morning. I was determined to get on a flight that night because I had something to do in California the next day, so I simply asked at the airport if they could get me on any other flight. The man who was helping me was kind enough to see if he could work it out and he found a flight that was leaving that night from the other airport in New

York City, but the only ticket left was in first class. As soon as I heard that, I had an inner knowing that I would be in that seat. So I waited while he asked his manager and the manager said no, they couldn't get me on that flight because the seat cost thousands of dollars more than the regular ticket I had purchased. I politely asked again, and I thought, "You know, why not? If there's only one seat available and I was supposed to be on a flight, then I *should* be on that one, right?"

I just kept asking.

Now here's the thing: I didn't get upset, or worked up, or angry. I was calm. I knew that I was going to get that first-class ticket. I had the expectation. So once the manager said no a second time, he left me a clue. He said, "I'm sorry, ma'am, but there is a phone number you can call for the airline." I thanked him and I sat down and phoned the airline and spoke to a really nice woman. I asked again. She tried to work it out for me, but she said, "I'm sorry, there's nothing I can do for you."

I wasn't angry or upset. That would have shifted my vibration. I simply said, "Thank you so much for trying. Can I speak to one of your managers? I'm more than happy to wait." I waited 20 minutes to be connected to her manager, and guess what? He got me on that flight—first class! I was in a seat that was better than the one I would have originally had if my flight hadn't been canceled. It was a beautiful seat that reclined completely into a bed. I had movies. I had amazing food and first-class service. I was really taken care of, and I had a wonderful flight.

Not only did I get my first-class seat, but once I got to California, I had a little layover from L.A. to San Francisco overnight and they put me up in a hotel. Why? Because I asked.

If I hadn't asked, I wouldn't have received the hotel room.

There's a beautiful power in receiving a no and then asking if there might be an alternative way that your goal could still manifest. It might be slightly different from how you'd imagined it to be, but you'll see that there could be a new direction that you're meant to go in. And you'd never have known if you hadn't stayed calm and asked for what you desired.

How to Apply It

When you receive a no, ask yourself where you can find another alternative. How can it still work out in your highest good? As William Ury, co-founder of Harvard's program on negotiation, states in his book *The Power of a Positive No*, instead of being reactive, be proactive. Listen attentively. Be respectful. Keep asking from a place of trust. There is another way to a greater yes.

In your manifestation journal, take some time to reflect on a no in your life that led to a yes that was even better than what you thought was possible. How did a new possibility open up for you when you received a no? Remember that situation the next time you receive a no and you'll be empowered to ask in a new way in order to receive a yes. Keep asking and keep going for that beautiful dream of yours.

Part 6

DELIGHT:
REAP THE REWARDS OF YOUR MANIFESTATIONS

Enjoy the process of manifestation. It's not simply about an end goal, but about the journey. Here you'll learn how to delight in all that is already there for you, and enhance your daily practices in order to step into greater abundance and happiness. Tap into your intuition to receive guidance for easy manifesting. Delight in creating wealth. Learn how to stay present and in a high vibrational place so that you truly become what you desire. Delight in being a powerful manifestor.

Follow Your Intuition

"Your sixth sense should be your first sense."

Sonia Choquette, New York Times *bestselling author and spiritual teacher*

Pay attention to your vibes and trust your gut.

We all are born with intuition. The information is like a radio wave that you can't see—all you have to do is tune into that frequency to listen.

Using your intuition is like strengthening a muscle: When you pay more attention to intuitive guidance, you get better at receiving information. When you're looking to decipher a yes from a no, you can use your intuition to decide. How can you tune into your intuition? Get quiet for a moment and ask your higher self if the decision "feels" right. Make the space to tune into your intuition. If you're having trouble figuring out which is your intuition and which is your mind getting in the way, go with your first instinct. This is almost always your intuition. It's that gut feeling you have. And it always feels lighter. You can even use this to sense things about other people around you. Have you ever walked into a room and felt a shift in energy? Once you start paying more attention to your intuitive guidance, you'll get better at receiving information. All you have to do is tune into that frequency to listen.

Remember our synchronicities exercise. If you're journaling synchronicities daily, this too increases your intuition. You should always trust your internal guidance and pay attention to life's synchronicities!

How to Apply It

Get clear on your yes and your no. A yes feels lighter in your body. It feels free. It feels warm and fuzzy. A no usually feels heavier. It feels draining. It might even feel like a knot in your stomach.

Start to tune into what a full-body yes feels like by asking yourself a question you know the answer to. If you know it's a yes, you can close your eyes and experience how a yes feels in your body.

Then ask yourself a question that you know the answer to is no. Close your eyes and feel the difference in your body. Feel the no. What area do you feel it in? How would you describe it?

Remember these distinctions so that you can easily use your intuition the next time you have a big decision to make. And when you use your intuition, you're easily guided by the universe and have a much easier time manifesting because you're able to receive information that's coming to you—just like the radio frequency.

Manifest Money

"What I know is, is that if you do work that you love, and the work fulfills you, the rest will come."

Oprah, talk show host, philanthropist, and founder of the OWN Network

Pay attention to your money and it will grow.

Chances are that money plays a key role in your big dream. If you're one of those people who thinks that you can't be spiritual or ethical *and* make money, think again. The more money you have, the more change you can make in the world.

One of the biggest questions I get all the time is how to manifest more money. And as a spiritual person, you may find yourself putting up an unconscious block to bringing in more because you feel guilty. So before I get into how to manifest more money, start to reframe your beliefs around accepting more. Start with this thought: The more money you have, the more change you can create in the world.

Money is simply an idea of value. It's a medium of exchange that's been rooted in livestock, grains, chocolate, shells, coins, paper money, and now virtual credit. Like everything, money is energy. You bring in what resonates with you as your worth. Money is not power. It's simply a tool for exchange. There are a lot of ways to make money. But it's important to always come to money from a place of playfulness—a place of delight. You can create money by giving something that's perceived to be valuable to someone else. It's easy to make money! There's no limit to what can come to you if you're in tune with it, if you call on it, and if you resonate with it.

If you constantly tell yourself that you can't afford things, you're in a scarcity mindset. Even if you don't see the physical proof of money in your bank account, you need to feel as if it's already there. So, try to get out of the habit of saying, "I can't afford that." If you say that you can't afford it, you never will. Instead, ask how you can afford it. Start to recite affirmations telling yourself that you have an abundance of money. That it flows easily and often.

Then, state your intention for what you want to do with the money. Money is a means to something else. So if you have an idea of how you'll use it, you'll be more likely to manifest it. It's not just a random number you decide you want to make. Rather, what will you do with it, and how much will that cost?

As you work to manifest money, keep in mind that money loves attention. Take a look at the money you have right now. Think of your money as your great love. You are in a relationship with your money. How would you treat the love of your life? Are you viewing your money in a nurturing way? The more attention you can give to your money, the more it will grow, so take the time to organize your finances and see how much money you have right now.

How to Apply It

Get out your manifestation journal. If you have debts, write down the specific amount of money you owe for each card, or each loan. Put a minus sign in front of the money you owe. Underneath, list every bank account you have and how much is in it. Add in any other investments, stocks, and bonds and write their amounts to the right of them. Then total them up. If you don't have any money on your credit cards, great! Now you know how much money you currently have. This may seem scary at first, but it's actually really empowering.

Next, set up a budget. Try to incorporate habits that nurture your money. Remember, if you pay attention to it, it grows. Understand how much you need to thrive right now. I like to create a budget on my computer. That way I can easily update it each month. But first, start with your manifestation journal. Then you can transfer your numbers to your computer for easy updating. Look at all your monthly expenses and list them out on the left side of the paper. Then write in the amount on the right side. Total up all of your expenses. This is how much base income you need to make each month. It's actually really liberating to know your numbers. From here, you can set a goal to bring in more so that you can save and splurge. You can write in expenses for things you want to manifest. That way you're making space for the money to come in. For example, you have a new car you want to buy. So you add the car payments into your budget now. Money is constantly coming to you and flowing out of you in a beautiful, positive, and organized way.

Advanced Manifesting Tip

Watch your language around money. Try to get out of the habit of saying, "I can't afford it." If you say that you can't afford it, you never will. That's a scarcity mindset, and you manifest what you believe. Your words help influence your subconscious thoughts. So begin to tell yourself that you have an abundance of money—that it flows easily and often. The next time you catch yourself saying, "I can't afford it," instead ask yourself, "How can I?" This opens it up to possibility rather than a definitive no. When writing your budget, use words that make you feel good! Instead of using typical words to describe the way you spend your money, make it abundant. For rent or mortgage, say "sanctuary." For groceries, say "delicious organic food." Have fun with it! Start telling yourself that "It's easy to make money!"

Decide How Your Money Will Make You Feel

"Abundance is not something we acquire.
It is something we tune into."

Wayne Dyer, philosopher, self-help author, and motivational speaker

Start with the end result and do things that make you feel abundant right now.

As I mentioned in the previous entry, simply having a random money goal is useless. You have to decide what you'll actually do with your money and why you want to manifest that much money into your life. For example, do you want to:

- Buy a house
- Pay for your children's education
- Take a vacation
- Pay off your debt
- Donate to a cause you believe in

Money is a means to something else. So if you have an idea of how you'll use it, you'll be more likely to manifest it. Set your intention for what you want to create in your life. There's no limit to what can come to you if you claim it and resonate with it. Imagine now that you have already manifested the money.

How will having the money make you feel? And more specifically, ask yourself how you'll feel when you have that thing your money provided for you. For example, when you're on vacation you might feel happy, lighter, free, abundant, etc. Once you know the feeling associated with the thing you want, you can start doing things right now that make you feel that way even if you don't have the money. By starting with the feeling, you begin to manifest more circumstances and wealth that are in alignment with that feeling.

How to Apply It

First determine how much money you want to manifest for the things you want to have or experience. Then set a non-negotiable commitment and make it believable. Start with something that may be a stretch for you, but that you believe you can manifest. You can always manifest more. If you say you want to be a millionaire but you're currently only making $30,000 a year, your money goal might feel too unrealistic. So your subconscious mind will block it. Instead, reach for a goal such as making $100,000 a year. Begin there. Then create an affirmation to go along with it. For example, you could say:

- "I make at least $10,000 a month."
- "I'm grateful I get paid well to do the work I love."
- "My clients pay me on time in full."
- "I always pay my bills before they're due."

Once you've created your affirmation, all you need to do is commit to your goal. Figure out how much of something you need to sell, or how often you need to work in order to make that happen. Come up with a plan. If you want to make $10,000 next month, but can't imagine how that will happen, it won't! Start imagining and make a list of all the ways you can bring in money right now. For example:

- E-mail my friends and family about the services I could provide in exchange for money.
- E-mail my friends and family and let them know I'm looking for a job.
- Call an old employer and ask if they need any extra help over the holidays.
- E-mail an old client who you loved working with and ask for a testimonial. Check in and see how she's doing. She might want repeat work. And if not, ask if she'd be willing to refer you to two of her friends.

There are a lot of ways to make money right now. You just have to open up to the possibilities. Wealth is a state of mind. You are already abundant.

Advanced Manifesting Tip

Clean out your wallet and your purse. If your wallet is stuffed so full of receipts that you have a hard time closing it, you need to organize it and file your receipts. This is a place where systems can help. Maybe every Friday you go through your wallet and file your receipts. Maybe every Monday your look at all your bills. If you have a purse or a briefcase, it needs attention too. A cluttered purse is a sign of a cluttered mind around money. So empty it out and organize it. You may even want to invest in a new purse or wallet. Find something that makes you feel glamorous and wealthy every time you use it.

Have a Wealthy Mindset

"I am one with the Power that created me. I am totally open and receptive to the abundant flow of prosperity that the Universe offers. All my needs and desires are met before I even ask. I am Divinely guided and protected, and I make choices that are beneficial for me. I rejoice in others' successes, knowing there is plenty for us all."

Louise Hay, bestselling author of
You Can Heal Your Life *and founder of Hay House*

There is more than enough financial abundance for everyone.

Delight in knowing that you are wealthy already. Your mindset is the most important factor in acquiring wealth. Money is a flow of energy. So it's constantly coming to you and flowing out of you in a beautiful, positive, and organized way. Think of it as a fun game to play. You can do whatever you put your mind to and you have the power to achieve anything. Seek out the support you need. Wealth grows as you continue to learn and grow. So keep expanding upon your beliefs and habits. Have fun and have a wealthy mindset, and your wealth will follow!

Think of your money as your great love. You are in a relationship with your money. How would you treat the love of your life? Try to incorporate habits that nurture your money. Pay attention to it, allow it to grow. All the wealthy people I know track their money. There are many ways you can track what's coming in and what's going out. You want to look at your numbers on a regular basis. Get to know them intimately. You can:

- Start a free Mint.com account to keep all your finances organized. If you're not familiar with it, it's an amazing resource that will send you reminders when your credit cards are due or when your bank accounts are getting low.
- Write down how much money comes in at the end of each day. I use a piece of paper for every month and number it 1–31 for the days in that month. At the end of the day, I put in how much I received. If I received something else of value, but not money, I put that in as well.

You want to do things that wealthy people do, not things that financially unstable people do. Look at the people you know around you. Who can you look to for good money habits? Try to spend some time learning their ways. Think of it this way: Rich people play the game on offense. They're in it to see how many goals they can score. Poor people play the game on defense. They're struggling to get by instead of looking at all the ways they can create wealth. Which side do you want to be on? If all that you want to do is pay the bills and be comfortable, that's all you'll ever manifest. Remember, it's all in your mindset! You can be rich *and* generous. And if you don't know any wealthy people, you may want to dive deeper and hire a financial advisor or a money coach. Seek out the support you need.

You are worthy of financial abundance. And there are many ways in which you are already abundant right now. How are you abundant in other ways? For example, you may be abundant in:

- Love
- Success
- Family
- Happiness
- Clothing

You may not have all the money just yet, but if you focus on what you do have, you'll begin to feel more abundant. And that feeling is going to bring you more abundance. Simple as that!

How to Apply It

Track your abundance! For each month, number a piece of paper 1–31 for the days of the month. Then create a column to the right with what you received, and a third column to the right with the value for each gift. On the top of the page, set a money goal for the month as a written affirmation. At the end of each day, write down what you received and its value in its corresponding row. Total it up at the end of the month and you'll most likely notice that you're receiving way more than you'd imagined. The first month that I started tracking my abundance, I made more than $10,000 that month. And I never would have known if I hadn't tracked it. The first month you do this, there may be a lot of zeros on different days. That's okay. Keep with the practice and your wealth will grow. Pay attention to your abundance and it will bring in more abundance.

Advanced Manifesting Tip

In your manifestation journal, write down all of the ways in which you are abundant right now. You can even add this to your daily gratitude practice. Recognizing that you are already abundant and being grateful for your abundance helps bring in more abundance.

Be in the Present

"Forever is composed of nows."

Emily Dickinson, poet

Focus on what you love about your life right now.

I'm sure you're familiar with the famous expression: "Yesterday is history. Tomorrow is a mystery. And today? Today is a gift. That's why we call it the present." It's true! The more you can give your attention completely to what you're doing at this exact moment, the more joy you will have, and the more desires you will be able to manifest.

Today, I invite you to delight in staying in the present moment as you go throughout your day. Try not to get caught up in thoughts such as "I should be working on my project" or "I still need to write my affirmations." Put down your cell phone. Leave it in your bag instead of on the dining room table. Enjoy the time you spend with your loved ones *now*. Who knows when you'll have this beautiful opportunity to connect in person again? Be in the moment. Trust that by being in the present moment, you are actually increasing your vibration, and this leads to more manifesting.

Manifesting is not all about doing. It's about believing in yourself and trusting that without a doubt, your dreams are manifesting. Staying in the present and giving your all to each activity makes a huge difference in your life. Whether it's doing the dishes, playing with your child, or working at your day job, by being the best at what you do in each moment, you'll see amazing results. You will become happier, feel more fulfilled, and start attracting the right people and "synchronistic" circumstances that will help support your big dream. Try to look at seemingly mundane activities and see possibility and wonder in how you can make them even better. How can you infuse joy into every moment? As we discussed in the "Pay Attention to Your Language" entry in Part 1, switch "I have to" to "I get to!" For example, "I have to do the dishes" becomes "I get to clear my mind while I do the dishes." "I have to take the train to work today because my car is in the shop" becomes "I get to read a book and relax on my way to work." You get the idea. This will help you remember that everything in your life has a beautiful purpose.

Try not to get caught up in holding onto things that have happened in the past. The more you can release old grudges and just enjoy yourself and the people you are with, the happier and lighter you will feel. For example, spending time with family may bring up hurtful reminders of incidences from the past. When you feel yourself going to a negative place, just think of what you're grateful for in that moment—think of something beautiful that you love about the person you're with and shift that negative into a positive. Even if someone's hurt you in the past, each moment brings a new opportunity for a fresh beginning. The same thing goes with yourself. If you're feeling bad about habits you've had, such as overeating on the holidays—and you notice how that doesn't make you feel good—recognize that today is a wonderful opportunity to start a new habit of only eating the amount of food that feels good and nourishes the *future* body that you envision. You will feel better!

In the same respect, you want to let go of any worry or anxiety you have about the future. Trust that your big dream is happening. You are already taking action. Now keep the belief there and stay present in what you're doing now. Give yourself love today. Be kind. You are doing amazing work! You're in exactly the right place. You are manifesting your dreams, exactly as you are meant to do.

How to Apply It

Go for an adventure for a few hours today without your cell phone. You might want to take a walk in nature. Go to a local park or botanical garden. Or just go about your day as usual. Whatever you do or where you go, just leave the phone at home! Stay present in whatever it is you're doing and pay attention to the experience. If you're going for a walk, pay attention to the way the wind blows through your hair. Notice any synchronicities you see. Practice gratitude for everything you notice—whether it be someone's smile or the sun warming your face. If you're going about your day as usual, notice how it feels to stay present without your phone. Did you notice anything new as a result of your greater focus? What are you grateful for in the moment? Notice how much more present you are to your life when you aren't distracted. Feel grateful to be alive. Then write about your experience later in your manifestation journal. Writing about it brings greater awareness. Have fun!

Practice the Art of Receiving

"Ask and you shall receive."
Abraham-Hicks, spiritual guide and channel

Open up to the gifts that are already there for you.

You're receiving all the time whether or not you realize it. You now understand how to ask for what you want in the right way to manifest it. Now I want you to pay attention to how you receive.

Notice how you react when you receive a compliment from someone. Do you shrug it off? For example, someone says to you, "I love your dress!" Do you say, "Oh, this thing? I got it from a discount store for $2." Or do you say, "Thank you!" and fully own the gift of the compliment?

It's interesting to notice how you are at receiving. If one of your dreams is to speak to large audiences, yet you cringe when you receive compliments, you're sending mixed messages to the universe. You say you want one thing, but your behaviors show the complete opposite. In order to manifest what you truly desire, you want to make sure your signals are clear.

I noticed recently that I was shoving away abundance. And I didn't even realize I was doing it at first. My parents are so giving and supportive. And they absolutely adore my daughter. So much so, that they constantly send her gifts to show their affection. We often receive packages once a week from them with a new outfit or art supply just because. I found myself getting annoyed by all the presents. Wasn't it wasteful? Who needs all of this stuff? I wanted them to "Just. Stop. Sending them."

And then I realized what I was doing.

I was actually stopping the flow of abundance because my focus was on being annoyed by the gifts, and not on being grateful for receiving them. When I noticed my behavior, I was able to flip it around. I affirmed how grateful I was that my parents were so giving. I wrote it in my manifestation journal. And then my gratitude expanded.

I've actually found that a lot of people I work with are, in fact, great manifestors. They're just not good at receiving. They complain about the gifts they're receiving. Or they don't think they deserve them, and shove them away. They feel guilty for receiving. All of this blocks the flow of abundance. When you do those things, you literally repel all the gifts that you receive.

The universe is constantly showering you with gifts. You just need to shift your perspective to see them, and open up to receive them with gratitude.

How to Apply It

Spend some time outside in nature today. I like to do this in the form of a silent gratitude walk. While you're walking, notice the abundance around you. It could be simply receiving the abundant gifts of nature—the sun, the flowers, the fresh air. And if you do receive a gift or a compliment, accept it with a grateful heart. Receive with love.

Advanced Manifesting Tip

In your manifestation journal, write down all the gifts that you received this month, then this week, then this year. Notice how you feel and then practice gratitude and appreciation for all that you have. You are an excellent receiver.

Practice the Power of Giving

"The true meaning of life is to plant trees, under whose shade you do not expect to sit."

Nelson Henderson, second generation farmer

The more you give to others, the more you receive in return.

The law of reciprocity is the law of giving and receiving. Giving is such an important step in manifesting abundance. The more you can give to others, the more you will receive in return. There are many ways to give.

Many successful people talk about tithing, the art of giving a percentage of your profits to charity. A lot of people give 10 percent of what they make, but you need to do what feels right for you. And don't feel that you have to wait until you have enough money to give. That actually delays your receiving. You're telling the universe, "I don't have enough. And therefore I can't give." And the universe, being reflective, will therefore continue to support your belief that you don't have enough.

What are the rules of giving that you should practice?

1. Give for the pure joy of giving.
2. Don't expect anything in return.
3. Remain unattached to how the recipient will use your gift.
4. Remember that the universe often rewards you from a different direction.
5. Remain open.

So give! But not out of obligation. Give because it makes you feel good. Give because you delight in giving. The cool thing is that when you're giving, you're naturally in a state of abundance. You trust that the universe is infinitely abundant and that there's more than enough for everyone. You'll notice that when you're in scarcity mode, you tend to hold onto your money. You aren't generous. And therefore, you aren't in the flow of abundance. But when you give, you know that more of it will return to you in other ways. By giving, you're keeping abundance in motion. And remember, movement is the natural order of the universe. The cells in your body are constantly moving and flowing. Abundance wants to move and flow. You don't want money to stay stagnant around you. You want your money to circulate. There are a lot of ways to give. It doesn't have to be financial.

Ask yourself, "Does my big dream serve others?" If you haven't already added a service or giveback component to your dream, now is the time. For example you could add something like:

- I start a nonprofit.
- We donate a portion of our proceeds to our favorite nonprofit.
- We have a volunteer day with our family.
- I go on a philanthropic trip with my love.
- We host community nights once a month.

You don't need to wait until you're "successful" to give. You can give a small amount of what you have now. Your resources for giving will grow along with you. And giving doesn't have to be purely financial. You can give love or support. You can volunteer your time.

How to Apply It

Write down a list of five causes that you feel strongly about. Then go back and circle the one that resonates with you the most. If this is difficult for you, think of something that upsets you so much that it motivates you to help. Ask yourself how you can give either your time or your money to the cause. It should be a thing that you feel good about doing—and something that fits in with where you are in your business and life right now. If you own your own business, perhaps it's donating a portion of the proceeds from a certain product to an organization. Or maybe you spend an afternoon volunteering somewhere. Perhaps giving for you is in the form of mentoring someone else who's just starting out. There are infinite possibilities for giving. And you don't have to have much to give. Even the smallest gestures have profound impact, like that dollar you put in the tip jar for the struggling musician on the subway, or holding the door open for a mom with her baby and stroller.

Advanced Manifesting Tip

Practice one random act of kindness today. Do it just to give, not to expect anything in return. And better yet, do this daily! There is great power in being generous and seeing value in everyone and everything else around you. The more you can lift others up, the more you will raise your own vibration. Even the smallest gift can leave an enormous impact. Don't doubt your own power to give. Each morning when you wake up, say "How can I serve others today?"

See the Good in Everyone

"If you judge people, you have no time to love them."

Mother Teresa, Roman Catholic nun

We are all connected spiritual beings who come from the same universal source.

Delight in knowing that everything is connected and you are a part of the good in the world. When you can approach everyone in your life from a spiritual perspective, you see that we are all spirits moving and operating in physical form. If someone does something that challenges you, you can make the conscious decision to react in a loving way. For example, just the other day I was riding my bike with my daughter in the baby seat behind me. There was a car behind us that was eager to turn as we crossed the street. We had the light and the right of way. The car beeped loudly at us to "hurry up." And it hurt my daughter's ears. With her hands cupping her ears, she said, "Mommy, why did that car beep at us?"

And I said, "Because the woman driving the car was in a hurry and was mad."

"Why was she mad?"

"Because she wasn't happy. And when people aren't happy, we need to send them love."

Sometimes the simplest ways we explain things to our children are the ways we need to remind ourselves to interact with the world around us. Truly, if we can silently wish everyone we meet love, peace, and happiness, the world will be a better place.

Instead of getting agitated by a situation at work or home, approach it as a spiritual observer. Most of the time, a negative situation isn't about you. It's about someone else. And if there is a lesson for you, you're able to fully receive it when you observe the situation. If you react out of haste, you're unable to receive and fully integrate your lessons. As a spiritual observer, you'll remember that all is well. You don't have to be affected by the outer chaos around you. Instead, you can bring your meditation practice into real life.

How to Apply It

Ask yourself, "How can I live with even more love in my heart?"

When you find yourself in a situation for you to be an observer, see the other person with a curious heart. You can intuitively ask yourself why the other person is behaving that way. Try to put yourself in the other person's shoes and see what her intention is. What's her block? When you can relate to other people on a spiritual level and react from a place of love and understanding, it helps remove any judgment toward them. And this, in turn, helps you love yourself more fully. This doesn't have to happen in difficult moments. There are opportunities every day to be more loving to others. Start with making eye contact with strangers and smiling. Say hello. You'll begin to notice how connected we all truly are. Conversations may start up, showing you more synchronicities and opportunities for manifesting. We all are a part of the same moving universe. And when you love someone else—even a perfect stranger—you are in fact, loving yourself.

Be Love

"When we form heart-centered beliefs within our bodies, in the language of physics we're creating the electrical and magnetic expression of them as waves of energy, which aren't confined to our hearts or limited by the physical barrier of our skin and bones. So clearly we're "speaking" to the world around us in each moment of every day through a language that has no words: the belief-waves of our hearts."

Gregg Braden, New York Times *bestselling author*

Listen to your heart and take every action with love.

Have you ever looked at the tasks that you want to accomplish, and they seem so huge? Almost impossible. It can feel overwhelming at times.

But if you have an idea that you want to pursue, there's an innate desire motivating you to act on your idea and work to realize your dream.

When I reflect on my life, I realize that all I've ever gained has been because I've had the courage to take a leap and step into the unknown for a simple desire that I had. I chose love over fear. And I did it again and again. Love is your natural essence, just as it is for me. And it is from that trusting place of pure love that miracles occur.

One of my favorite spiritual teachers on pure love is Amma. She's affectionately known as the hugging saint. *Amma* means "mother" in many languages and this woman lives an extraordinary life of service and selfless love. She's given hugs to more than 32 million people, many of whom waited hours in line to receive one. I've personally been hugged by her numerous times. I've even visited her ashram in India. To me, it's not just about the hug.

The magic lies in witnessing Amma sit for 18-plus hours a day hugging people, giving them comfort and love. She's attracted devotees who embody love. They've helped her start a nonprofit organization, Embracing the World, which is active in 40-plus countries, provides food, shelter, healthcare, and education, and has donated large sums of money to disaster relief. Amma is a living example of the power of love to change the world. With love, all your dreams can manifest. When you lead with your heart, other people will join forces with you to carry out your vision. Amma says, "Where there is true love, anything is effortless."

Loving others and sending love out into the world starts with self-love. When you love yourself, you are aligned with your spirit, and that's where effortless manifestation occurs.

It's no coincidence that the largest electromagnetic field produced by your body emanates from your heart. You see, the heart and brain maintain a continuous two-way dialogue, each influencing the other's functioning. According to the HeartMath Institute, a quantum physics research center focused on the heart, there is a flow of awareness, understanding, and intuition that we experience when the mind and emotions are brought into alignment with the heart. The more we pay attention to what we sense the heart is saying to us, the greater ability we have to access the intelligence and guidance that the heart brings to the table. Not only is this about listening to your intuition, but this is scientifically proven!

The greatest manifestation principle in the world is *love*!

If you can take every action with love, you'll serve more and you'll be more successful. You are love. The more that you can embody love, the easier it will be to manifest, and the more you'll be in touch with the universe and be supported to live out your dreams. When you return to a state of self-appreciation, when you feel love for your life, for all of humanity and nature, and most importantly, for yourself, the more life force there will be behind your desires and the easier it will be to manifest. We are all co-creating with the universe from a place of love.

Love yourself.

Be love!

How to Apply It

Place your hands over your heart, close your eyes, and take a deep breath. You are here in this moment. You get to experience all of life's joys in this body. Feel the gratitude and peace. Feel the love flood your heart and expand throughout your body, eventually radiating out into the world around you. Focus your intention on the present. Smile. Ask for any guidance from your heart and listen for the answer. Go back to this place whenever you need to simply by placing a hand on your heart as a reminder.

Advanced Manifesting Tip

Write yourself a love note—a real handwritten love letter. In it, share all the things you love about yourself. You can literally mail it to yourself, or keep it in a place where you can refer to it often. I suggest placing it in your wallet or on an altar at home. This will serve as a beautiful reminder of just how special and powerful you are. You *are* love.

Conclusion

"You are very powerful, provided you know how powerful you are."

Yogi Bhajan, spiritual teacher

It's my vision that when we all realize our true power and step into our own light and our own greatness, the entire planet will shift. Even if your dream is not to change the world, just living out *your* big dream or living in *your* light has a huge ripple effect. I really see this book as a way to help shift this entire planet so we can all be happy, conscious manifestors, co-creating with the universe. And if we can all be the light for the others in our lives, how amazing would that be?

Just by being you and embodying love, manifesting from your heart, you can be an example for those in your life, and that's huge! You are going to inspire them to shine their light brighter.

There's a reason that you found yourself reading this book. You are meant for greatness. Look at it as a synchronicity in your life that you are here, that this book found *you*. That you are being guided and that your dreams are possible, and you are manifesting and things *are* beautiful. The world is beautiful. The universe is abundant and so are you. You are resourceful, you are worthy, and you so deserve it. You make your dreams possible. Your dreams are real. I am grateful for *you*. Here's to co-creating with the universe together and manifesting all that your heart desires.

To help you manifest with ease, I invite you to join our free community at www.facebook.com/groups/manifesteasy/. When you are in a community with other people who are manifesting together, sharing their gratitude and accomplishments, it actually helps you stay positive. You raise your vibration for manifesting. I found this over and over again in the programs that I teach.

Keep using all the tools from this book. I've given you an abundance of new information. You can take the time to go over any lessons from previous parts, or feel free to start from the very beginning. Each day presents a new opportunity for growth and learning. You are manifesting with ease.

Index

About the Author

Jen Mazer is the Queen of Manifestation. She's always been able to dream up outrageous adventures and actually live them out—from rubbing elbows at a small private cocktail party hosted by Martin Scorsese, to living rent-free in the East Village of Manhattan for 10 years, to paying off over $38,000 of debt in less than a year, having her artwork published in the *New York Times*, traveling the world, meeting the man of her dreams (a successful rock star), giving birth at home to a beautiful daughter, and starting a green school in Africa. Jen is a sought-after transformational speaker and coach. She teaches people how to manifest their biggest dreams while making an impact on the world. She is known for her signature Manifestation Masters Program and Private Success Coaching. Jen is the cofounder of the new board game for women, Sparked, available now. She has interviewed some of the world's biggest thought leaders through her series Manifesting with the Masters. Learn more at www.queenofmanifestation.com.